14

DAY
BOOK

Setting the Stage

*This book is a 2017 selection in
the Driftless Connecticut Series,
for an outstanding book in any field
on a Connecticut topic or written
by a Connecticut author.*

SETTING THE STAGE

What We Do, How We Do It, and Why

DAVID HAYS

WESLEYAN UNIVERSITY PRESS · MIDDLETOWN, CONNECTICUT

Wesleyan University Press

Middletown, CT 06459

www.wesleyan.edu/wespress

© 2017 David Hays

Manufactured in the United States of America

Designed by April Leidig

Typeset in Garamond by Copperline Book Services, Inc.

The Driftless Connecticut Series is funded by the
Beatrice Fox Auerbach Foundation Fund
at the Hartford Foundation for Public Giving

Library of Congress Cataloging-in-Publication Data
available upon request

5 4 3 2 1

CONTENTS

ACKNOWLEDGMENTS

THIS BOOK IS DEDICATED TO Peter Feller, Willy Nolan, and Arnold Abramson; to Ron Bates, Joe Harbuck, and Charlie Bugbee; and to hundreds of other men and women I worked with to build, paint, set up, focus, and run all those plays, musicals, and operas (and the brassiere commercial).

Many thanks to thoughtful and helpful readers: first, Lary Bloom; then my Nancy and my daughter, Julia, and son, Dan; and Laine Dyer, plus Harry Haskell, Rick Horning, John Guare, Peter Walker, Jess Maghan, Dick Buel, J Ranelli, Howard Fishman, Joel Grey, Tandy Cronin, Glenn Barenbeim, and Chita Rivera. And Martha Kaplan and Suzanna Tamminen and Susan Abel, with gratitude.

Setting the Stage

CHAPTER ONE

Read This

T HIS IS A BOOK about stage scenery, with notes on lighting, and how they work, with thoughts on the how and the why and the good and the bad. The designer, and I am the designer in this case, is woven into the complex tapestry of skills and personalities that create a theatre event. Incidentally, I spell "theater" with an "-er" to mean the building, and "-re" to mean the craft or industry. If you plan to be a designer, this book will be helpful. If you are to be a writer or director or actor or producer or critic or audience member, perhaps this book will add to your understanding of that man or woman behind the curtain.

I taught for over fifty years at New York University (NYU), Columbia, Harvard, Wesleyan, and the National Theater Institute. This is the book I would have assigned to my students. You will find passages explaining how a setting was conceived and executed, thoughts about how to express your-self to a director or producer, and some stupidities to avoid; and I will con-vey a sense of the life you might lead if you choose this profession. There are other books that delve more explicitly into technical skills — how to stretch canvas, how to build platforms or folding steps — and I recom-mend them. But read this book first.

I'm writing about work devoted to giving actors, singers, and dancers a milieu, a surround, an ambience, and about being part of the teams that forge our noble craft. I designed for drama, for musicals, for ballet, for modern dance, for opera, for brassiere and whiskey commercials, and I designed and consulted on theater buildings.

The names of some talented men and women I worked with are preserved on film or tapes, such as Arthur Penn — *Bonnie and Clyde* and *Little Big Man;* or Elia Kazan — *On the Waterfront* and *East of Eden.* Some giants of my time, Sir Tyrone Guthrie for example, left no such record, and unless you are a certain age, you may not know of them. Time has passed. I will name some former co-workers. I want the air to hear their names again, famous or not. They deserve it; we deserve it; the air deserves it.

CHAPTER TWO

Starting Out

B EFORE PLUNGING INTO an account of the first successful
Broadway play I designed, let me say a word: On the first day of
my first job — I was thirteen — I gave an enema to a goat. This
was in 1943, farmhands were fighting the war, and for ten dollars a week I worked at a dairy farm. I've often thought of that first sunny
afternoon and I've been encouraged. Nasty work, but the goat was relieved,
perhaps even pleased, and I was an effective soldier in our war effort —
a proud member of a team.

Good luck followed, and I will come to that. What I want to do now is
to speak of the first successful Broadway play I designed. This may seem
abrupt, but it serves to introduce the thought process of designing LONG
DAY'S JOURNEY INTO NIGHT. This was a remarkable opportunity for a
young designer to support the work of Eugene O'Neill, thought by many to
be our greatest American playwright. (Note the word "playwright." Plays,
we say, are wrought, not written. We write and direct, design, act, dance,
or sing: we develop our work in process — with others.)

CHAPTER THREE

Long Day's Journey into O'Neill

I WAS A NEW RESIDENT of New York City. During the day, I was painting scenery at the old Metropolitan Opera House on Thirty-Eighth Street, and at night I was designing, building, painting, and lighting at Circle in the Square. After a superb production of Eugene O'Neill's THE ICEMAN COMETH — with a breathtaking performance by Jason Robards — José Quintero and his partner, Leigh Connell, artistic directors at the Circle, approached Carlotta O'Neill and convinced her to let them produce LONG DAY'S JOURNEY INTO NIGHT. O'Neill had asked that it not be performed until twenty-five years after his death, but Mrs. O'Neill relented. Her early release was high drama, and there was great buzz about the production. Fredric March would play the father, James Tyrone; Jason Robards, the older son, Jamie; Brad Dillman, the younger son, Edmund (representing O'Neill); and Florence Eldredge, Mary, wife of James and mother of Jamie and Edmund. This is essentially a four-character play, but there is a fifth — a maid, Cathleen — not a major role, but to be well played by Katherine Ross. I would design it, for which I am eternally grateful to José — but that didn't add to the buzz.

O'Neill sets the play in a small sunroom in the New London, Connecticut, home where the family lived when not on tour. The father is famous to the public for his role in THE COUNT OF MONTE CRISTO and to his family for cheap hotel rooms and fried-egg sandwiches. The playwright's stage directions call for a room with a back wall, an entrance to the rest of the house on both sides, and windows on the walls that come downstage on each side. (One of the ironies of my life is that twenty years after this play, I lived in this very house for three years with my family. O'Neill's memory of that small room was exact, surely engraved in his mind by pain.)

This is a long play — four acts — and whatever variety we could achieve in the one room would be precious. José Quintero wanted to depart from the sacrosanct instructions. The visual point of the play, he said, was the movement from a cheerful morning light through noon, then a foggy afternoon, then a dark and depressing night. The stage directions gave us an interior back wall, not the commanding and informative moods of daylight, then darkness. I worked out a set with a huge bay window spanning the entire back wall. It could logically embrace a low platform, lifting upstage actors so they could be seen more easily over the heads of those downstage. Also there could be window seats, actually chests, the kind of sit-on boxes that are jammed with skates and tennis racquets and so forth in a country house. These would be built-in places to sit, relieving us of finding yet more furniture in a room that should look barren and uncared for. These details may seem unimportant and premature considering the major service of the big windows, but even small details with the "aha!" factor make you sense that you are on the right track.

Step by step. I first united the windows in a curve across the back wall. But the floor plan, or ground plan — how a set looks as seen from above — has to have vigor. Weak corners weaken the picture and are sensed by the audience. I had briefly worked for the designer Boris Aronson, converting his setting for THE DIARY OF ANNE FRANK to a simpler and smaller set for the road company. He insisted on this principle and, as usual, he was right. So next I set the three windows not on a curve, but as a bay window unit jutting out of the room, framed with sharp corners.

The windows couldn't be bare — that would feel too naked. But shabby curtains to reflect Mrs. Tyrone's poor housekeeping? That's Halloween, too suggestive of cobwebs and bats. Mrs. Tyrone states, in Act I, "I've never felt it was my home. It was wrong from the start. Everything was done in the cheapest way." As the play proceeds, we see that she is incapable of significant improvements.

I asked my teacher Ray Sovey for help with these bare windows, and he suggested colored glass squares, typical of those early years of the twentieth century, rimming the upper pane of the double-hung windows. To me, these colored squares were the best thing on the set. In the morning, they glowed, as hopeful, pretty light streamed through them. At noon, they supplied color; in the fog of the third act, they were muted; and at night, they had that bleak blackness of a church's stained glass when seen from outside. Years later, I lectured on this process at Harvard. After the lecture, two distinguished professors came to me, one of them actually in tears, and said that my request for help from my old teacher had so deeply touched them. No former student had ever asked for their help.

Now for the rest of the ground plan, starting with the two upstage entrances O'Neill calls for. Here his exact memory of the room overcame his ordinary common sense. There is simply no reason for two entrances, one to a rarely used front parlor, the other to the dining room. Years later I saw Olivier's production of this play in London and he followed the stage directions exactly. Two entrances (archways, not doors) plus the wall between took up the entire upstage, and the value of changing light as the play progressed was lost. I used a single archway on the upstage end of the stage-right wall. The bay window is at right angles to this wall, angled itself; thus the bay slants downstage toward stage left, ending in a narrow screen door. Thus a center line to the room is sensed — it is as if we cut across a room at an angle. This is not easy to visualize, so I've included a simple floor plan.

Concerning furniture on the set. Around the central table were appropriate chairs: a heavy Morris chair for father, a wicker rocker for mama, and ordinary side chairs for the sons. The three bears — plus one. O'Neill calls for three wicker chairs, but I felt the differentiation was better in its small way. My main source for these items and others, such as a chandelier and water pitcher, was the 1912 Sears Roebuck catalog.

In the play, the father is generally rooted to his chair. The sons occasionally take a seat, but usually roam the whole room, particularly the restless Jamie during his bitter speeches. Mary Tyrone uses her rocker, but there was also room on the set for a wicker chaise longue, and it was a good variant for Mary.

In describing the furnishings, O'Neill makes a point of two bookcases. The father's would contain classics such as Smollett's *Complete History of England,* Gibbon's *History of the Decline and Fall of the Roman Empire,* and so on. The younger son's would contain Marx, Wilde, Swinburne,

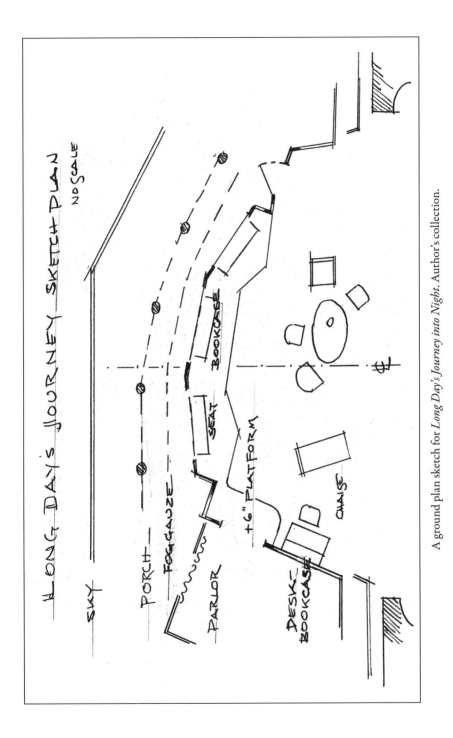

A ground plan sketch for *Long Day's Journey into Night*. Author's collection.

and Kipling. Easy to show precisely, if a director chose, on a film close-up. The best a designer can do on the distant stage is to show one collection in leather bindings, the other in paper. And why not? Why not execute the playwright's simple request in this case? We ignored or altered plenty of his suggestions. But then, how much does an audience see? Do not expect people to notice and analyze every detail, such as this choice of books. Yet the details build up. How many rooms do we enter and sense that they are just right, even at first glance?

In this instance, the bookcases play a role, separating the generations. In Act IV, the father growls to Edmund, "Where do you get your taste in authors? That damned library of yours! Voltaire, Rousseau, Schopenhauer, Nietzsche, Ibsen! Atheists, fools, and madmen! And your poets! This Dowson, and this Baudelaire, and Swinburne and Oscar Wilde, and Whitman and Poe! Whoremongers and degenerates! Pah! When I've three good sets of Shakespeare there."

One problem was to find room for these bookcases. The father's bookcase could be a low built-in under the center bay window, between the chests. I felt that Edmund, representing O'Neill, should have a desk, a literary base in the room in contrast to the older, rootless brother. More about furniture choices later. But the stage-right wall, where I put his desk, was narrow. The solution was to put the bookcase on top of his desk, making it into a so-called secretary desk. I wanted him to have a wicker desk, similar to those often seen in seaside hotels, glass-topped, with a back rim of cubbyholes holding hotel stationery. It would look light, appropriately misplaced among the heavy furnishings, a summer note in a winter room. But there were no such desks in wicker, none that replaced the low cubbyholes with a three- or four-tier bookshelf. Trust me. But couldn't there be? You shouldn't fool around carelessly with great classic styles like Louis XIV or Chippendale. But some styles, such as Queen Anne, are more informal, and coffee tables (not known in her lifetime) have appeared; even flush toilets (also not known to the queen) are dressed up in her style, with seat covers incorporating fake wicker insets. These seem fair game, even if they somewhat pollute the style's purity. So I reasoned that Mrs. Tyrone had simply gone to a local wicker maker, common artisans at that time, and ordered this piece for her son. No one complained.

Outside the windows I placed porch posts, vines, and a decorative rim running below the roof. This made sense because of the fog needed for Act III. How could you show there was fog without having something for the fog to conceal? To create this fog, we lowered a scrim (gauze curtain) between the windows and the porch posts and vines, and that scrim gauzed away the outside world. I also enjoyed the porch decoration because the roof rim was the only piece of the O'Neill's actual house that we copied onstage.

Robert Edmond Jones, a designer who worked with O'Neill, liked symmetry, and he influenced the playwright. Designers can do that. I was once handed a play requiring six sets, with turntables. I saw no reason that it couldn't be played on one set, and that was done, with the playwright and director's agreement, thereby saving a ton of construction and operating expenses — and enhancing the play. My set was carefully described in the stage directions of the play when it was published. A student asked me years later, "So what did you do but exactly follow the playwright's directions?" Expand this thought: the playwright also gleaned credit from others who worked on the first run because many of his poor speeches were cut by the director or producer, and some of the play's best moments were inspired by them or by — yes — an actor.

O'Neill, surely influenced by Jones, calls for a table centered in the room. This is the gathering point of bitterness, anger, and guilt, centering the whirling accusations. José did not want it centered. It would be a tennis game, he noted: you look right, you look left. So the table wasn't centered. However, because of the angles of the set, the perceived center line suggests that the table and the chandelier above it are centered in the room. Of course, this is an illusion — they are off-center, toward stage left, as José wished.

An electric cord plugged into the chandelier above the table ran down to a small lamp on the table. A nice touch asked for by O'Neill, indicating cheapness to a modern audience, who have a profusion of wall or floor outlets. As for the table itself, the trouble was that the round table called for in the stage directions caused sight-line problems. I discovered this while drawing it in the plan. The actor sitting at the upstage center of the table was hidden from the side audience by the heads of the actors seated at the sides of the table. The solution was to make the table oval, to shrink its up- and downstage measurement. This brought the upstage actor downstage a foot or so, enough to make him visible from the side seats. Easy. The table still looked round, and if it didn't, so what? Years after this, José wrote in a memoir that he had instructed me to make the table oval. I was surprised that he had even noticed the alteration. I brought this up in my next conversation with Jason. "That's the mildest of stings," he said. "José took credit for inventing—and then instructed me on—every acting idea I ever had."

Downstage left, I put a screen door leading out to the porch. There was a notion that the father would be seen sneaking along the porch as he goes to the cellar to get more whiskey, but this looked comic and was cut. The screen door was never used, and José didn't like the way I initially positioned it. He wanted it facing more toward the audience, to serve as a background for much of Mary's third-act speech in the foggy afternoon. So I nipped six inches from the bay windows and angled the door. Her speech is so sad in the enveloping gloom of the fog-bound afternoon, and it offers a strong contrast to the vitriol of the men: "You're a sentimental fool," she says, alone on the set. "What is so wonderful about that first meeting between a silly romantic schoolgirl and a matinee idol? You were much happier before you knew he existed, in the Convent where you used to pray to the Blessed Virgin."

Tharon Musser lit this play beautifully. I lit the rest of my plays, except one where I was fired and one other with Tharon. Tharon and I became close friends, and we often consulted to find solutions to scenery or lighting difficulties. After I started my own company, the National Theatre of the Deaf, I did not always have the time to spend on lighting. A set designer can design a set, oversee the building and painting, see it set up out of town, and visit from time to time. But the lighting designer is stuck for days and days setting levels. There were three shows during these years that I designed but did not light, because I was too involved with my own company to spend that time. Two went well, and the other badly, lighted by a man who was only concerned with his own effects — the kind of effects that would display his genius.

One interesting lighting problem we worked through on LONG DAY'S JOURNEY was the unlighted formal living room, upstage right, showing slightly behind its archway entrance into the main room. How to make a dark room? Just leaving it unlighted usually does not work onstage — it looks as if you failed to attend to it. What we did was to open the heavy drapes in the room about two inches and shoot bright sunlight through that slot. Just before curtain, the electrician went into the room and slapped a loaded blackboard eraser. At rise, the chalk dust caught the slanted beams of light, contrasting with the darkness behind, and the effect was fine. The dust settled, of course, illustrating that an effect well made at the start of a scene can serve throughout the scene: it remains in the audience's consciousness even after they become involved in other matters.

Another note on lighting: At the end of the play, midnight, the three men are around the table. Jamie is in a drunken sleep. His father is drunk but knows what's about to come. Edmund is alert. The father says, "I think I'll catch a few winks. Why don't you do the same, Edmund. It'll pass the time until she —" Suddenly the living room light snaps on and Mary Tyrone comes through that archway, ghostly in flowing white nightclothes, carrying her wedding dress. "Suddenly" is the word, bringing a gasp from the Boston audience. In New Haven, for switchboard convenience, Tharon made that lighting unit larger — going from a 500-watt lamp to a 1,000-watt lamp — and hooked it to a dimmer. The dimmer handle was swiftly lifted — but not as swiftly as the snap-on we had in Boston, and the larger lamp took a small fraction of a second more to reach full brightness. Because of this tiny difference we lost that gasp and caused a murmur instead, as if the audience noticed the effect rather than being struck by it. Tharon corrected that, of course. Small differences can make big differences.

Other productions were mounted during our run, and our assistant stage manager showed me a photo of another set. "Isn't this great? No ceiling!" he untactfully crowed. The picture itself was interesting, the set similar to mine but indeed no ceiling. The lack of a ceiling signals imagination to some, but I'm not sure it worked well in this case. The ceiling contained the drama of the play; one looked out of the trapped, or trapping, room. Opening the room to the sky frees it — too much, in my opinion.

I was praised by Brooks Atkinson of the *New York Times*, our reigning critic, as an "excellent setting of a cheerless living room with dingy furniture and hideous little touches of unimaginative décor." Walter Kerr of the *Herald Tribune*, second only to Mr. Atkinson, said the set was "a perfect echo — curving and empty — of the universe these characters wander."

WHAT I LEARNED

Some of O'Neill's stage directions added to our sense of the room without being of practical use. Remember that O'Neill was writing at the end of a tradition where plays were often read at home in evening gatherings — home entertainment before television. (The vestige of these now-rare gatherings is the book club.) To add to these evenings, the playwright might engage us with an extended description of the town and customs of the area. Read Bernard Shaw's CANDIDA to understand this.

In fact, one learns more about the scenic needs of a play from a close reading of the script than from a playwright's instructions. Some designers actually avoid reading all stage directions. The designer is hired as an inventive partner, and all ingredients, including the anticipated strength of an actor, should be stirred in the pot. Yes, do what the playwright wants, but, like the director, try to add more to the production and steer away from mistakes.

I was once involved in a conference with the playwright Sam Shepard and the superb costume designer Pat Zipprodt (FIDDLER ON THE ROOF, CHICAGO, THE GRADUATE, and on and on). Sam, just before he stalked out of the room, stated furiously that costumers often didn't do as he instructed. "But," said Pat, "if you choose an actress that looks sickly in the black you specify, I'll dress her in another color. Or if you insist on black, get another actress."

A note about velour, a cloth used often to cover stage walls, as in this set: It's essentially a cheap velvet, easy to paint, although it's important to be aware of the nap — think of stroking a cat the wrong way. You've probably seen this painted velour technique used less subtly in Mexican restaurants, with a matador dressed gaudily in yellow and gold, waving his red muleta against a background of black velour or velvet. In the case of this set, I used a stencil to make a faint, rather worn-out wallpaper pattern. The color was a muted green, the tone of the walls slightly heavy, heightening the contrast with the windows and the scattered furniture.

In the theatre, we usually apply the cloth with the nap pointing down so that the cloth more readily absorbs light bouncing up from the stage floor, rather than reflecting it.

Ceilings to these so-called box sets are not, in my experience, made of velour, but of ordinary canvas or linen. They reflect much of this bounce from the floor, and so are painted darker than you might expect. When sets are retouched before opening, you often see the painters darken the ceilings even more.

If only we could stop light after it has done its job on an actor. The bounce that I mention on the walls and ceiling makes set and lighting designers crazy. So we fuss and fuss with focus and framing to pull the actors out of the background. As for box sets, often thought of as rooms with one wall removed so that the audience can see into them, Willy Nolan, a truly wondrous builder of stage scenery, said, "Don't knock that missing wall. It's my profit!"

I learned the value of every person's contribution both from my work and from a course I taught at Harvard to help future audience members understand who does what. Guest lecturers from all the disciplines — producers, directors, actors, costumers, writers of incidental music, and more — came to Cambridge and explained what they brought to the table. To be sure, the playwright and the actors are supreme, but the composer of almost unconsciously heard incidental music may be a greater genius, and he's doing his best. I mention this here because we can learn so much from teaching. It organizes and clarifies our thinking, and I would urge anyone who has a leg up on this — or any career — to teach. (Teach well, of course. I had a friend who taught that comedy used wavy lines and tragedy used straight lines. Nonsense.)

"Survival time" occurs when one member of a team abandons the big picture and goes off on his or her own, usually because the production is sinking and he (or she) will not go down with it but launch his own lifeboat. This desertion defeats artistry in our industry. Joseph Conrad wrote with authority in *The Mirror of the Sea* that such behavior destroys art: "He was not genuine in this display which might have been art. He was thinking of his own self; he hankered after the meretricious glory of a showy performance."

A warning to young designers: No matter how supportive your work is to the production, someone in management is going to say, "You know, your stuff doesn't sell one more ticket." Suck it up. They still want scenery. I enjoyed some exceptions to these foolish remarks, and creative criticism and appreciation from Hal Prince, Robert Whitehead, Fred Coe, Cy Feuer, and almost all of the people in ballet and opera, where "the picture" is more important to them.

We took the play to a festival in Paris. There were fine scene painters there, and some old crafts survived. The wicker maker, for example, took my design in stride. The next year, our production played in London. I did not go, but was disappointed in one way when I saw the photographs: the four chairs around the table were not the chairs you would find in a New England seaside home. But consider this: these British chairs meant more to London audiences in creating the "three bears" family than mine. Brits have their own seaside styles, and the recognition of father, mother, and sons' chairs was more vivid to them this way. A small point but worthy of attention. Interesting. Was I more responsible to honestly show a foreign audience what an American home looked like? Or was the obligation to make the differentiation of the chairs as clear as possible to the audience on their own terms?

Small things make big differences, as I learned from the lighting of Mary's dramatic midnight entrance. I remember a tiny moment from Olivier's London production, a dozen years later, when Olivier, as the cheapskate father, is asked the time. He takes out his pocket watch, the old-fashioned style with a lid, opens it about a half-inch and peers in, then snaps it shut. He is so stingy he won't let out the time. A good note, something we remember, something magical. As a teenager, I saw Eddie Dowling, in the epilogue to THE GLASS MENAGERIE, play a merchant seaman. With a clap of his hands, he flips a cigarette into his mouth, along the way bouncing it off his pea coat sleeve and spinning it in the air. A brilliant detail. Skill like this is so valuable. Don't we go to shows and athletic events to see superhuman events?

Here are some further things to ponder when considering using a ceiling in a set. As mentioned, I redrew Boris Aronson's setting for ANNE FRANK. His room for the people in hiding was beautifully done, but it also had no ceiling. Above the walls of the room, you saw a map of Amsterdam. Good thought, that the people in hiding were denied the freedom of their city, and this map reminds us of this. But actually — though don't take this too seriously — settings should inspire *feeling*, rather than *thought*. I would have suggested to the director a ceiling to the attic room that confined them, and one small window looking out to the sky. I would also suggest that having Anne silhouetted against it, looking out, might make a good picture for a curtain-up moment.

To see a contrasting "set," be sure to go to the magnificent memorial for the displaced of World War II, behind Notre Dame in Paris, if you've not done so already. There is no ceiling to the courtyard of the memorial, just high stone walls and sky above, with one small barred window looking out on the Seine. According to the theory I just described, this window alone, with a ceiling or roof to the courtyard, would have worked. And I think it would have. But in this case, the sky offering unattainable freedom over the high walls worked wonderfully. The moral is, as we say: what works, works. Do not get stuck on theories and principles.

Here is a story that marginally works for the "What I Learned" theme of this section, and I cannot resist telling it. I had been apprenticed to the designer Roger Furse in London, and we kept in touch. It was not long after London that my work in New York started and then LONG DAY'S JOURNEY went to Paris. We played at a festival in the old Sarah Bernhardt Theater (since renamed Théâtre de la Ville) in Châtelet. Roger was in Paris and I got tickets for him. After the play, he sat at the Café Zimmer with José Quintero. This meeting resulted in work for Roger, designing José's next film. I was pleased to have helped get a job for my old boss. During the course of that meeting, Roger commented on my setting and said, as I learned from José the next morning, "David was an eager young man and a good assistant, but now he's better than I am." The remark went through my heart like an arrow and still hurts. Maybe Roger was not sober, and yes, it was a good set. But could I draw like an angel? Did I have any feel for costuming? Could I do films? Why so much pain from praise? Should I recall Rex Whistler's "How sweet it is to get unjust praise from someone one loves"? Or did I learn that if our gods are to be torn down, let them not do it themselves?

My daughter, Julia, perceptive and pragmatic, chides me for my pain. "Dad, you have spent your life eagerly learning from masters, and now you are trying to pass on some wisdom. Your greatest pleasure is when someone you love exceeds you — think of your pleasure when your son or grandsons handle a boat more skillfully than you do. Would you deny Roger, a child-less man who cared for you, that same pleasure? Ache away, Pop, but think how much you may have pleased and rewarded him."

EXERCISE

Occasionally in these chapters I will suggest an exercise. The first one: Draw. Draw your hand. Try it palm toward you, fingers open, thumb across the palm. Practice this while you're on the phone, or instead of general doodling. My point is not to make directors or playwrights or anyone ex-cellent at drawing, but to sharpen your eyes. The good directors and play-wrights I worked with had at least this in common: they were wonderfully perceptive.

CHAPTER FOUR

Getting the Idea

D ESIGN WORK BEGAN for me in high school. Good luck was concealed as bad luck when I broke my collarbone playing football. (A grandchild speaks up: "Did you wear a leather helmet, Pop?") Unable to play the winter sport, basketball, I designed our two one-act Christmas plays. I forget the name of the first one, but the other, taking its cue from my future, was ILE by Eugene O'Neill. Mr. Harris, our history teacher, met me in the hall the next day and praised the work. "It looked good, David, and the shifts were well done." In that hallway, at that moment, my ambition ignited. Why not combine my enjoyment of drawing and model making with my other pleasure, literature? Or "stories," as I would have said at the time. True, another way to combine those pleasures might be to illustrate books, but we were a family that sailed, and the energy of the great moving canvas was happy to me. The work I imagined meant motion in three dimensions: performers moving in a space.

During my time in high school, my parents were taking me to great plays: I saw Laurette Taylor in THE GLASS MENAGERIE, I saw the original DEATH OF A SALESMAN, directed by Elia Kazan. Who would dream that I was to become Elia Kazan's designer? I saw SOUTH PACIFIC, and didn't imagine that I would later design two musicals for Richard Rodgers, or that I would sit in a Palm Springs garden forty years later, holding hands with the dying Mary Martin as she talked of flying. Not her Peter Pan flying, but the lift-off she knew would soon be happening.

The day after my encounter with Mr. Harris, I wrote two well-known stage designers asking for a moment with each. I mailed the letters on a

Tuesday, and Thursday brought both answers. (The mail was faster then.) I took the train into New York from our suburban home. Don Oenslager, soon to be my teacher and later a personal friend, advised me to go to art school. Robert Edmond Jones said that drawing and painting would take care of themselves, so I should go to college and study art history. "And," he added, "learn how to read." I often think of Mr. Jones and this surprising statement. He was right. Thoughtful reading is not easy. The second course is what I chose. The phrase "artists of occasions" comes from his superb book *The Dramatic Imagination.*

My college years at Harvard were the four best years of the Brattle Theatre Company in Cambridge, and I apprenticed for the company's designer, Robert O'Hearn. We were on a two-week rotation, so I worked on fifty productions. The Brattle was one of the first of the regional companies that sprang up in the fifties, along with companies like the Arena in Washington and the Long Wharf in New Haven. What a group in Cambridge! Albie Marre, Jerry Kilty, Jan Farrand, Nan Marchand, Bryant Haliday, Robert Fletcher, David Hersey, Fred Gwynne, Jean Cook, and more. There were appearances by guest artists like Hermione Gingold, Nancy Walker, and Zero Mostel (who was currently blacklisted and out of work).

By the time I graduated, I had been allowed to design three productions — and two were good. I was granted a Fulbright to study at the Old Vic in London, probably because Thornton Wilder, living that year in my dorm as he delivered a series of lectures, wrote a fine letter for me, surely mistaking me for O'Hearn.

WHAT I LEARNED

I learned the basics of building and painting and shifting scenery. I learned how to mix paint. In those days, glue came in a gelatinous brick that you melted in boiling water. Then you added powdered pigment. Too much glue in the paint, and the cloth drop would become too stiff too roll. Too little glue, and when you unrolled the drop the pigment would lie there in its original dry and dusty form. I learned other things:

If the scene shop is freezing in winter, offer it to the director for rehearsal. Heat will appear.

Get your stuff done! The actors need the stage; don't hold them up. Never open a door, even to a small closet, without knocking.

I started to learn to question, because directors didn't *always* know everything. I sometimes collected props for a production, and a visiting director at that time said to me, "David, we should have something symbolic on the mantelpiece." I said, "Sure. Symbolic of what?" Director: "Just symbolic."

I learned how utterly satisfying good work can be, and how rewarding it is to be part of a team that can make an audience laugh and cry. I learned how theatre exposes our inner selves, and how actors are our surrogates, our shadow sides, the Olympians of our emotions.

One of the productions I designed for the Brattle was Sheridan's THE CRITIC. The set used a false floor, just canvas, which was not meant to bear weight. Due to inadequate onstage rehearsal, Jerry Kilty indeed stepped on it and plunged down to chest height during a performance. The play is comic, and Jerry made the best of his fall. Afterward I went to him, almost in tears, and apologized. "Thank you, David," the gracious actor replied. "But you were weeping in private backstage. I had to deal with it in front of an audience."

I also learned that a small group working too hard can survive only so long. But when this company split up, and those involved went on to the brighter lights on Broadway, they all told me how wonderful it had been, and that they would have given up the fame and bigger paychecks if only the company could have lasted forever.

I learned the value of polished communication. My letters to Don Oenslager and Robert Edmond Jones must have been good letters for them to respond so quickly! Surely my parents helped me write them. When I lectured at theatre schools, students would often ask about the secret to success. I would surprise them — at least the technical crews — by telling them to speak well and write well.

Perhaps most important — and I did not recognize this until many years later — I became empowered. Empowering experiences are necessary to any artist: to the easel painter who for the first time is appreciated in some way, on and on. Here, at the end of my undergraduate work, with settings for Ferenc Molnár's LILIOM (the play was later transformed by

Rodgers and Hammerstein to the musical CAROUSEL), I made a powerful contribution to the success of a commercial play. Those twelve words — "I made a powerful contribution to the success of a commercial play" — could be the mantra for a lifetime of satisfying work. I was not an easel painter or sculptor, solitary artists, but a member of teams — lively, engaged teams with joyful hopes.

EXERCISE

Draw a room in your house or apartment. Include a door and a window, some pictures on the wall, and perhaps a view from the window. Now pull up Piet Mondrian's works on the Internet and study his paintings. Adjust your drawing. The rectangular shapes will take on new meaning.

CHAPTER FIVE

London, the Glorious City

I N THE FIFTIES, we regarded London as the greatest theatre center. Since in London the stage work was in the city and filmmaking was in its suburbs, an actor could work on a movie during the day and appear onstage at night. Stateside, where Hollywood had succeeded in luring film many miles from New York, the disciplines are more segregated. We had fine plays by then, by O'Neill, Wilder, Tennessee Williams, and Arthur Miller, but Shakespeare and the classic playwrights of the seventeenth and eighteenth centuries reigned in London.

I started my Fulbright year in London by painting scenery at the Old Vic, center of classical theatre. I was assisting John Collins, who painted in thin build-ups of transparent color. It was not the most glamorous time to be in London. We were still rationing, London was a pile of rubble, and it was freezing in the paint shop. On one wall we painted a huge Tudor fireplace and a roaring fire, and that helped keep us warm.

Roger Furse (who designed Olivier's films of HENRY V and HAMLET, and the two CLEOPATRAS brought to Broadway in 1951) was designing THE MERCHANT OF VENICE for the Vic and was running late. I could draft construction plans. I was sent to help. (I was on a federal grant and cost nothing for Roger and the Vic.) That began a year of delightful assistance and friendship.

From Roger's scene sketches (or "renderings"), I made cardboard models of the set, including furniture if needed, and we'd modify them as needed. Then I created accurate architectural drawings for the builders. I also outlined the individual units of scenery on good illustration board and Roger would color them for the painters.

We worked in his seventeenth-century studio in Chelsea. Among my projects was drafting the original scenery for THE MOUSETRAP. That show is still running, more than sixty years later. (After a meeting about THE MOUSETRAP, Roger complained, "I asked for a small weekly royalty, and they refused. Oh well, what the hell.") I also drafted THE SLEEPING PRINCE (directed initially by Alfred Lunt, taken over by Olivier).

Roger hated meetings. He came back to the studio one afternoon, grumbling about wasting two hours on King Arthur's round table. "If it's too small, we can't get enough knights around it. If it's too big, we can't get the cameras around it."

I bought a bicycle and raced about the great city. My roommate was Norman Geschwind, who became one of the great neurologists of the past century. One reason I loved wondrous London was its magical fogs, and during my spring there, in 1953, the last of the great "black fogs" fell on us. Truly, your hand was dim in front of your face. Theaters closed because audiences couldn't see the stage. Even on normal days, a thickness in air held the city. Men and women were merely shapes, the city of Johnson and Wren and Baker Street was cloaked. After that black fog, burning soft coal was banned. In years to come, when I went over to visit or to mount one of my shows, the clean city lacked that mystery of my youth, that smell of burning stone, and I was disappointed. One especially disappointing afternoon, the new owner of Roger's home and studio refused a visit from my wife and me, and I discovered that the cozy pub across the street had become a French restaurant. But that evening, on that same city street, we saw a fox climb an eight-foot garden wall. An omen? Sudden magic? Roger's spirit? Though the connection is not entirely logical, this moment makes me recall the most marvelous of all stage directions, in Act II of THE CHERRY ORCHARD, during a picnic. In Stark Young's translation: "Suddenly a distant sound is heard, as if from the sky, like the sound of a snapped string, dying away, mournful." Something unexplained, haunting.

At the Vic, I also met and assisted Leslie Hurry, a superb — and crazy — designer. Perhaps, he said, his mind had been affected by growing up above the family mortuary. Leslie didn't have a studio, but knelt by his bed and set a pad of paper on it to draw. He slowly built up his sketches, like John Collins, though he used transparent inks rather than paints. One of my jobs was to take a fresh pad of paper and make a small wrinkle or smudge on every page. Leslie couldn't face the challenge, the unlimited possibilities, of a blank or, as he said, "virgin," page. During the war, he had stacked a dozen paintings in his room, and a piece of shrapnel tore through the center of the stack — leaving gaping holes in a dozen canvases. At that moment, he told me, "I got an immediate stabbing pain in my thigh, and it's never gone away."

Here's a valuable comment from Leslie Hurry. Director: "Leslie, you've just contradicted yourself." Leslie: "So what?"

WHAT I LEARNED

One of the principal things I learned in London: do not slurp your tea to cool it.

I also learned not to begrudge the praise and recognition of others in your field. Alfred Lunt visited Roger almost daily to watch the set develop for THE SLEEPING PRINCE. He would end these meetings by describing his experiences with other great designers: Oliver Messel, Eugene Berman, even Christian Bérard. I said one day, after Mr. Lunt left, "Doesn't it annoy you, Roger, how he praises these other designers?" Roger replied, "Nonsense, David. He'll praise me just as much next chance he gets."

We continued that show for Olivier after Mr. Lunt left (or was asked to leave). As usual for Roger, we were somewhat late. We were hard at work playing pinball at the Eight Bells, the pub opposite Roger's house and studio, when Sir Laurence himself walked in. Rather than giving a craven apology for our moment of leisure under pressure, Roger barked, "Hah! Caught! And badly!" A good lesson; a good reaction. I have not used it enough.

Roger wanted me to stay another year, and asked Olivier to write my draft board for an extension. Can you imagine my small-town draft board opening a letter from Lord Olivier? It was written, and Olivier handed it to me, the envelope open. "May I read it?" "Of course, dear boy." I read the letter, thanked him, and sealed the envelope. "No, dear boy, this is how you should do it: take the unsealed envelope, thank me, then with a flourish" (he demonstrated this flourish), "seal it *unread.*"

Roger taught me a useful basic technique: When you make a sketch of your proposed setting, draw it carefully, then put on a free wash of color. *Cover the whole sketch* when you do this. You can "cut it up" (define the details) later, on this base. Again, when you draw and color a rendering for a set, work all over your paper, don't get stuck on a detail—do those last.

I learned that if you have the proud title of "assistant" or "apprentice," you run, you do not walk, to your assigned jobs, and whatever is asked, you do—even if it is the middle of the night. Today the word "apprentice" seems to be replaced by "intern," a position that is still unpaid, but with a higher-class title.

From London, I was able to travel to Spain, France, Germany, and Italy, and I learned to stand in front of a painting or sculpture for an hour of study. (I cannot do that now, but if you are a student reading this, do it.)

EXERCISE

Do exactly what I did in those Fulbright days: Stand in front of a painting for a full hour. Try a complex painting, perhaps a Bruegel or a Bosch or that great Seurat in Chicago. Then try simpler but equally profound works (there are too many to mention). Keep in mind Elia Kazan's comment: "It's hard, but not complicated."

CHAPTER SIX

Yale and Green Mansions

ETURNING FOR GRADUATE study at Yale was gloomy. New Haven at that time was not Boston, Cambridge, or — believe me —London. It has improved in the last sixty years. I plugged along, doing weekly projects, and I learned. Don Oenslager taught set design and was a good critic. "I get the color of blood and guts, but why put them on rags, David?" That was a MACBETH. He fiddled with our renderings, and one day he held up a handsome watercolor by my roommate Bob Drumheller. "Needs more motion in the sky," he said, and held the delicate drawing under the faucet in the classroom. With an awful SKKRACKKK, water spurted out all over the rendering, and Don held up a blank square of cardboard.

Our costume instructor was Frank Bevan, and for an OTHELLO production, I reasoned that Iago, the cold, scheming man, should wear ice blue. Mr. Bevan held up my sketch. "What kind of a designer," he said — and right there, mid-sentence, my hope to design costumes withered —"would dress Iago in baby blue?" Later in the year, reviewing all my work, Mr. Bevan said that I was a romantic. I asked what that meant. "You have more than food in your belly," he said.

That summer, I inherited a job held by a classmate the year before, and so became the set designer at Green Mansions. This was an Adirondack summer camp, where singles (mostly) went for a week of sun and water and, they hoped, sex. City people could pee in the woods. This was before jet travel to the Caribbean or Europe. The notion of going to a bar and meeting someone for sex that very night was just getting under way (as was "the pill").

This was before air conditioning in theaters, and most closed for the summer. Green Mansions was also a theatre camp. It had been the formative home of the Group Theatre, with Elia Kazan, Cheryl Crawford, Clifford Odets, Robert Lewis, Lee Strasberg, John Garfield, and others. Now we, the camp theatre staff, were expected to deliver original plays or revues and good musical revivals twice a week on the camp's small stage. Charles Strouse, Lee Adams, and Michael Stuart were in residence. The producer was Mickey Ross, later responsible for much of *All in the Family*. My work was good enough, but speed was needed and I became somewhat of a minimalist, supplying what George Balanchine later often asked for: "as less as possible."

The best thing about that summer was that I met Leonora, my future wife, who was working at Green Mansions as a dancer. I went up to camp two weeks early with the technical crew to get a jump on the frantic season. The singers and dancers arrived one week early. Their first night was spent trying on the season's costumes, some of which were skimpy. I was painting a drop for BRIGADOON onstage, the only flat space available. The dressing rooms were below the ancient stage and the thin muslin cloth of the backdrop. I heard, "Shit, I'll have to shave." We were married that December.

WHAT I LEARNED

In my group of graduate students, I paid close attention to their struggles, their successes, their failures, and they watched mine. A good way to learn. Some of those lessons were

Never talk behind a drop. Careers have been spoiled by criticism or anger expressed behind what seems to be, but is most definitely not, a soundproof wall. Don't be so angry anyway. A theatre career is a tough and exhausting. Do something else if you blow up or burn out too easily.

Someone yelling at a performer "Back out!" meaning "Get back onstage," can be easily confused with "Blackout!" which startles your switchboard operator into a decisive wrong action.

Graduate study is rarely happy. Architecture students seemed cheerful and medical students were too busy to misbehave anyway, but in the so-called liberal arts, the future was and is clouded. Unemployment has always loomed in theatre, and not all theatre-school graduates stick with it. They became, in our lingo, "civilians."

Again, make the stage ready for the performers. At Yale at that time, technical crews dominated the work. Performers did not take the stage until we were damn ready for them. I didn't like that; it wasn't realistic preparation.

Words kill. Is it "baby blue" or "ice blue"? I recall a handsome arch designed by Rouben Ter-Arutunian that had a rough surface, as if garnished with seashells. Some wit described it as "the garlic arch," and it never made it to performance.

Mr. Bevan said that he was as interested in quantity as quality. What? Quantity? An insult to a young artist! But I was wrong. Stage designers are not independent artists, not easel painters who can show their work when they want. We work with others, at speed, and our favorite schemes can be vetoed by the director or producer. Then we have to adjust or start again. If you feel that you'll never again catch the mood you depicted in a certain drawing or painting, perhaps you haven't done enough drawings or paintings in your life. Perhaps you are not confident, or experienced enough. Frank Bevan was right. This came home to me simply when I remembered a high school baseball game. At the plate, I was startled by a beanball, so at the next pitch I was nervous and backed away a bit from the plate. If we had played more games and practiced more, I would have taken the beanball in stride.

EXERCISE

Look at an ordinary and familiar object, perhaps a chair. Draw it, even crudely (no one's looking). Now turn the object upside down and draw it again. You may be surprised that you draw it more accurately. At least, you may see it more clearly. Use this as a reminder to draw (or see) what is truly there, not what you *believe* is there.

CHAPTER SEVEN

Boston Again, and Tanglewood

WHILE I WAS at Green Mansions, friends from the Brattle phoned. Would I come to Boston and be a teaching fellow at a new theatre department at Boston University? I would earn a salary and get a master's degree at the end of one year. The faculty would be Sarah Caldwell, Horace Armistead, Ray Sovey, Elliot Norton, and David Pressman. Add the excitement of a new venture. Of course I went.

I ran student crews, supervised the refurbishment of Sarah Orne Jewett's old theater, and designed and painted. I found an apartment near Charles Street station, and when Leonora joined me, she participated in all the programs. She became pregnant, and that became suddenly apparent as she was performing Laura in THE GLASS MENAGERIE.

That summer, I designed at Tanglewood, working on, among other works, ZAIDE for Sarah Caldwell. This is a short, unfinished opera by Mozart, and I set it in an Asian garden. A simple projector threw an image of clouds on the set's cyclorama. The projector sat on the stage floor behind the garden wall and, forgetting all warnings, the tenor sat in front of the projector, waiting for his entrance. His sharp image, as he picked his nose, was thirty feet high in the sky.

Tanglewood's opera department at that time was led by Boris Goldovsky and Sarah Caldwell. They were brilliant artists, and I recall some amusing conversations. A singer, after auditioning, asked, "Suggestions, sir?" Boris: "Zip your fly." A patron complained, "Mr. Goldovsky, opera is so fake. The diva is dying, but is able to ruminate at length and at full volume." The maestro responded, "Why, you are so ungrateful! You are not interested in her final thoughts? And you think she should sing them so softly you can't hear them?"

WHAT I LEARNED

Horace Armistead and Ray Sovey were superb teachers, and it was instructive to make up the new rules for an academic department as we went along. Stupid ones: there should be separate faculty toilets. Wiser ones: how much individual attention to give to lagging students.

As the stage renovation supervisor, I learned that dust does not stop growing after a height of one inch.

Check the lighting booth. There is probably a graduate student living in it.

Some performers, whatever their gifts onstage, don't have common sense backstage. Part of a designer's job, though it is usually handed over to the stage manager, is to protect the actors from tripping over cables, strolling absentmindedly onto the stage, or picking their noses in the virtuosic manner described above.

Explain, explain, explain. You don't want a director saying to you — despite showing him drawings, plans, and even a model —"David, you never told me the platforms were *raised*!" (Yes, that happened; you can't make that up.) A similar story. There's an old joke: "Can we have funnier lights?" That was actually said to me! I hope it's never said to you.

Now a sad story. Sarah Caldwell did not like the orchestra to be seen. In one of the operas, based on O'Neill's THE ROPE, we stretched the floor cloth out over the pit, leaving a small hole for Sarah's head at the conductor's position. You could not see where the stage ended and the pit cover began — it was the same canvas. A film crew arrived to scope out the setup, and the director walked out onto the stretched cloth. Our warning shouts were too late. He made it out about six feet and fell with a cry through the tearing canvas into the deep pit. He was falling fast when his knee hit a music stand, and he lay screaming on the floor.

He should have sued, and he did. I wasn't blamed and wasn't involved in the suit, and I don't know the outcome, but I doubt if the unfortunate man ever walked normally again.

There is a point that always comes to me when I remember this misery. Safety of course. A fence, rope, or chain. But also this: looking down at the man through the hole in the canvas, I saw his brown and white tasseled golf-style shoes, highlighting the contrast of his debonair outfit to his writhing pain. It is still vivid to me; it knots my gut. The stark lesson illuminates the essence of much of our work: contrast.

EXERCISE

Learn to print attractively and clearly — all of you. In London, a friend of Roger's taught me. Letters should be the same height, and don't let your sentences droop. The main trick is to find a slant you prefer for the letters: straight up, angled, or even tilted backwards. (This is easy to maintain for letters with a vertical spine, like L or K, but harder for letters like A or O.)

CHAPTER EIGHT

Painting Lessons from a Virtuoso

H ORACE ARMISTEAD, my first boss at Boston University, had been a fine designer and a brilliant scene painter. He advised that the lay-in (first coat) should be free and easy, just basic shapes and colors. Move and splash it freely; it's just the lay-in. Then, when the lay-in dries, do the detailing ("cut it up"), and that's also free and easy because the lay-in was so good. "Also," he said, "don't lose the drawing." That meant don't slosh over and hide the careful drawing on the drop. (This first cover-all is reminiscent of Roger Furse's advice to me about doing a scene sketch in watercolor.)

During my Boston year, I also had the chance to work with George Lord. There were three scene painters in Boston, and two were named George Lord, though unrelated to each other. The third scene painter was "Burnt-Umber Charlie," also called "Sepia Sam," for the reason you can guess. He had a shop and rented scenery. "If the old stinker would paint more stuff, I could rent it," said his son. "If that damn kid would rent stuff, I'd have enough money to paint more," said the father. Pure Dickens.

The George Lord I assisted was an old man, but with a brush in his hand he was still a magician. He could dip one corner of a broad brush into dark green, the other corner into a lighter green, and with a rapid downward wiggle produce a tree, showing the sunny and shady sides of the leaves. Or, with different shades of green, dark shadow and moonlight. A few quick strokes and branches peered through. (We called the brushes he used "fitches," supposedly named after the animal that donated the hair.)

George had a repertoire of four trees, although he could paint any others, or anything for that matter, given a sketch or a photo or a picture cut from magazine. His basic trees were a birch, a pine or fir, an oak or maple, and an apple tree. Using the same two-color dip, he could also paint a variety of moldings, such as the classic egg and dart, with amazing wrist-wiggling speed. Then, with a smaller brush, he added some dark shadows and, if needed, highlights — again, with dazzling speed. See John Singer Sargent for stunning highlights, he advised.

George told me that before the talking pictures, there were fifty acting companies in the larger Boston area. He had painted scenery for many of them, and also for a firm that rented out scenery. He showed me their catalog. You could rent a "center door, fancy" drop, add a couple of potted palms, and there was your hotel or mansion lobby. Or you could rent a kitchen: "Country kitchen, wallpaper; city kitchen, paint," he said. There were dozens of landscapes and farmyards and terraces with awnings. He said that when you rented the sets for a show, if you chose to present one of the many plays in their files, they would also send along the scripts, perhaps full ones for the director and the stage manager, and "sides" for the actors. Sides were sheets given to each actor on which only his or her speeches were printed, with the cue lines preceding the speeches.

The marvelously painted backdrops might display painted chairs and tables so skillfully done that you might try to set down a package on them. The backdrops were lighted by strip lights, basically tin troughs with bulbs (or "lamps") screwed in every six inches or so. These gave an overall stage illumination that hit the drops (and the actors) flat on, and this lighting aided the illusion created by the good painting. But with more individually focused spotlights on adjusted stage areas, a development led by my first adviser, Robert Edmond Jones, real chairs and real moldings were needed. Trompe l'oeil drops with their painted shadows didn't seem to fool anyone any more — or to put it another way, we were no longer willing to be fooled.

I painted the ice for an ice show with George — big stars in red and blue, with outlines for the white stars. When we were done, the Zamboni covered our work with two layers of ice. We wore galoshes and kept our brushes moving. If you pause and your brush freezes to the ice, you end up glued there, idiotically yelling for hot water.

When I later came to New York, I painted at Chester Rakeman's studio on West Forty-Seventh Street and at the Metropolitan Opera, then on Thirty-Eighth Street. Neither of these facilities had floor space, and we painted on sturdy counterweighted frames, which we could raise and lower. The canvas drops were tacked to them. This was not as fast as painting on the floor. The area available at any one time was only seven feet high; you couldn't walk around on the drop and paint it anywhere; nor could you use some of the splashier techniques. Time was lost raising and lowering the frames. It was more difficult to snap the chalk lines that framed the squares that enabled you to enlarge a small sketch, with its small squares, to full size. At the Met, the two frames were far upstage, and a six-foot catwalk for the painters ran between them. The frames worked on the same rigging as the rest of the great overstage fly loft. If some joker raised both frames quickly at the same time, we were convinced we were falling and everyone screamed. On a positive note, while we worked, we heard wonderful music as the singers rehearsed.

WHAT I LEARNED

Painting stage scenery is a mix of speed and accuracy by fine painters as they enlarge the designer's images from his renderings. Arnold Abramson, in New York, was a superb painter and skillful at managing his talented crew. I was never a fine painter, but I learned how to describe what I wanted, what to expect, how fast scenery can be painted, how different it looks in the studio from its appearance onstage, and how to criticize without hurting anyone's feelings.

I learned some specific tricks, such as the way we can create a huge oval (say, thirty feet long) with a long piece of string, two nails, and a piece of charcoal. I learned that the fastest way to heat water is to plunge a live steam hose into a bucket of water. Later I saw that the well-equipped Imperial Theater in Tokyo had steam pockets downstage on both sides of the stage. Great for making dry ice mist quickly and abundantly.

George Lord told me that Thomas Rowlandson (1756–1827), a Brit best known for his satirical cartoons, was of help to him. "Look at his foliage," George explained. "There is a background smear of color, showing the general outline of a tree or stand of trees. Then see how in some of these color blobs, he paints a cluster of leaves rather exactly, and the eye expands that exactness and you have the illusion of a large spread of exact leaves."

George complained that directors and producers often saw his work before it was completed. "Never show a fool an unfinished work," he barked. I thought of this years later when I saw ballet dancers wearing thick and untidy wool leg warmers, as if to say, "I'm in rehearsal, obviously. You won't see these gorgeous limbs until I'm good and ready." Lesson: Beware of letting a director or producer see incomplete or indecisive thinking. At least offer thinking that is on a secure road to somewhere he can travel with you. Much of theatre is an exposed art, and I feel sorry for actors as they slowly build a character, with the usual missteps, in front of others.

Do not use this in a somewhat reverse way: too quick, too soon. I once asked a prop man for a set of fine (reproduction) bone china and was handed plastic plates. The intention was to make me a prima donna if I didn't accept them. That is where a friendly laugh is your ally. If you can't laugh at errors, choose other work — although I cannot name a profession that is immune from this advice.

EXERCISE

You've probably seen a painter, seated at an easel, hold a pencil or brush at arm's length to match the angle of a roofline or any angled object. Again, this is an exercise to improve your perception, not your knowledge. My students all profited by this, whether drawing a barn or a live model: angle of shoulders, hips, nipples (men have them too).

CHAPTER NINE

New York

WHEN THE TANGLEWOOD season ended, Leonora and I drove to New York, all of our belongings in the back of our old car. I took the exam to enter our union, Local 829. We are set and lighting and costume designers and scenery painters (and, at that time, paperhangers, but they didn't take this exam). This union is the key to Broadway work. We have rubber stamps with the union logo to validate our drawings, and the designers I've mentioned learning from are numbered in the single figures. I am number eight hundred.

I scored second among the thirty or so who competed in the exam, which consisted of a day turning out watercolor sketches of sets and costumes, plus a day in a paint studio enlarging, on a cloth, small drawings or photos handed to us. Leonora mentioned my second place to my father, who liked her. He was a prominent trial attorney, and he advised her to not say that again: "They'll find and hire the designer who came in first."

In rapid succession we then found a small apartment on West Sixty-Ninth Street and Leonora gave birth. That was nine months and six days after we were married. Leonora had wanted to dance for a few years before breeding, but we never regretted our marvelous Julia. "Conceived on the courthouse steps," said my mother. And then, concerned she hadn't been mean enough, she added, "First babies are often two weeks late." Leonora, a barefoot, Martha Graham–style dancer, represented the "floating world" to my mother, not the *"Kinder, Küche,* and *Kirche"* she wanted for me. Jews support the arts — but that meant earning and contributing money, and perhaps one should buy a season ticket, but certainly not engaging in the risky business of entering the field. But the grandchildren (Daniel followed) were a blessing and after some time mother forgave Leonora. Thirty years.

One day, wheeling the baby carriage down the street, Leonora met José Quintero. During our year in Boston, José had come to Boston University to direct three short Thornton Wilder plays, and I had designed the lighting. José's designer at Circle in the Square (who later became my assistant) had just had a breakdown. Was I available? Of course.

My first show was Gregorio Martínez Sierra's THE CRADLE SONG. This was followed by others, but the huge hit was THE ICEMAN COMETH. The old Circle in the Square was a haunting space. If you sat in the empty room, without scenery or actors, you could begin to see spirits rising and hear echoes of great speeches. Whatever made this happen — perhaps the proportions of the shadowy room — cannot be clearly explained. Perhaps the space carried in it all the signs, the history, of its use. If a director wanted a room like that, he would ask for a room "with meaning." Perhaps this would not be literal meaning, with a design that showed peeling wallpaper, with each layer telling us something (a palimpsest). This is intellect, not mood. What a designer would do with this concept is the essence of our craft.

Circle in the Square was a three-quarters stage, meaning that the stage floor was surrounded by seats on three sides. This theater, under Quintero's leadership, spearheaded the off-Broadway movement. Geraldine Page's performance in Tennessee Williams's SUMMER AND SMOKE, before I arrived, was a starburst on the scene in New York — and nationally, where small "open" performance spaces were being created. By "open" I mean that there is no proscenium.

The O'Neill revival was the idea of Leigh Connell, José's partner at that time. Leigh was quiet, gentle, and wise. THE ICEMAN COMETH began it, and as I noted in chapter 1, in that show Jason Robards emerged as one of our greatest stage artists. My set was good: The bar was at the non-audience end of the stage, with painted tiles and sawdust on the floor. Peter Falk, who later played Columbo, was the bartender. The street door, with an etched glass panel, was alongside the bar, and a shaft of sunlight could pass through that panel and stretch along the entire stage floor, carrying with it the entering actor's extended shadow. From a central dusty chandelier, a spider web of thin ropes fanned out over the stage and audience and attached along the side walls. There was a spray available that created cobwebs. The whole room and audience were embraced and involved. The door to the imagined upstairs (read Joseph Mitchell's *McSorley's Wonderful Saloon* and *Up in the Old Hotel*) was a beaded curtain, made from the rosary beads of the nuns in CRADLE SONG.

It was about this time that the curtain did not always go up to start the play. It might be up (or "out," as we say) when the audience wandered in, the advantage being that they could absorb the mood of the play in advance. There would be special lighting onstage to enhance this, then the house lights (auditorium lights) would fade and the stage lights would shift to support the play and actors. Of course such open stages as at Circle in the Square did not have curtains. Sitting under those spreading cobwebs was a fine start.

WHAT I LEARNED

Take a good look at the room where the play will take place. If you are going out of town, to Philadelphia or Boston or wherever, and know where you will end up in New York, look at that final house and imagine it. The total effect when the curtain rises is a good lining for your brain as you design. Perhaps, for example, the auditorium supplies a gaudy gold picture frame for the stage. And size really matters. We once had a good comedy playing in Boston's intimate Wilbur Theatre: Robertson Davies's LEAVEN OF MALICE, directed by Tyrone Guthrie. Then it died at the immense Martin Beck (now the Al Hirschfeld) in New York. I believe that if we had opened at the intimate Golden or Booth we'd still be running. If your theater is "off Broadway," this thinking is unavoidable, because each space, usually an open space, is different.

I learned to light such an open stage (no proscenium). An actor standing on the edge of the stage facing the audience is easily lighted from positions above the audience — but when she turns around, how do you hit the face?

Light on the face, from the best angle, would carry on into the audience's eyes. So you pick away at angles, from sides — and it sometimes works.

Another example of unusual space considerations: Ray Sovey designed the original OUR TOWN. Easy, right, since there was no set? Not so. The bare stage of the Henry Miller Theater was full of distractions — radiators and iron ladders and the like — and these had to be adjusted or carefully painted to blend in. And the basic question: Is it a bare *stage* that the play demands? Or a bare *space*? It's the former. Mr. Wilder wanted to challenge theatre tradition.

Another note on Thornton Wilder. At the end of my Boston year, I designed THE SKIN OF OUR TEETH for an outdoor production on the Boston Common. There wasn't much I could do on that platform, although I later learned how. The remarkable thing was that Mr. Wilder showed up, and we had a lively discussion. Can you imagine the thrill to a young designer? Wilder's point was that the house of the Antrobus family should reflect all styles of architecture through the ages. My thought was that this would be vague and drab, and we would fare better if we were to pinpoint a fleeting style like high Victorian. The audience would get it: how bright things rise, then fade away. I thought Mr. Wilder's idea would create a sort of permanent dullness, everything blended to make a bland soup, instead of emphasizing the ephemeral. So be specific! That is usually good advice. I have no memory of how we ended the conversation, but I suspect I received another Olivier-like "My dear boy," and a pat on the shoulder.

Concerning the author Joseph Mitchell, I am serious when I suggest readings like this to students. Learn to read, suggested Robert Edmond Jones. Design students should not just look at pictures. Read what is so often behind them. Good writing sits in your memory. Often, years after I've made a design, the source, subconscious at the time, will occur to me, and it might be literary as well as visual. Even sounds that enter your mental warehouse can influence design. Consider the surprising explosion of pigeons' wingbeats when you walk into an abandoned building. There's a color, a shadow-sense in that, a curtain-raising mood.

Teamwork is important. A team of painters is different than an athletic team, but not too different. You don't compete to win, but you do race time: the curtain will go up. You strive for the approval of the designer of the show, and should be a bit nervous when a respected designer shows up to look at what you have done. The key to my first jobs at Rakeman's and the Met was not just skill, but coordinated speed — yes, just plain speed, whether that meant me racing four flights to the bottom of the paint frame to hold the end of a chalk line, or quickly priming a drop with an eight-inch brush loaded with heavy starching goop. It was tiring but satisfying work for five or six of us, and the drops or set pieces or props we produced were often beautiful and always useful.

I mentioned that in the theatre, the curtain is "out," not "up." I use both "up" and "out." To the audience in a conventional theatre, the curtain is "in," or down, as they enter, then goes "out" for a limited time while they watch the play. (A great remark, attributed to George S. Kaufman or Groucho Marx: "I saw [the play] under adverse conditions — the curtain was up.")

Now, in most stage houses (the backstage) a drop flies *out* (up) into the flys. (I know, I know.) You might say it goes *out* of sight, and comes back *in* to sight. If you haven't got the height, drops can roll up like window shades and there are other tricks, such as "tripping," but that's another book. In my experience in Broadway theaters, the height is usually sixty feet, but the ballet and opera houses I've worked in go up to ninety, even one hundred and ten feet. That's a lot — but if your proscenium can open up to forty feet high, that's what you need. Of course, we all must work in houses where there are no flys at all, and miracles are expected for scene changes.

To stage workers in rehearsal or scenic set-up, the front or house curtain is always out for days or weeks. Finally the audience starts to enter, usually a half-hour before the show starts. It's surprising then for us to see the curtain in, and once we had so ignored it that just before performance we discovered it didn't work. After the show, the curtain stays in for perhaps fifteen minutes while the audience files out, then it is out again. Quite opposite to the audience experience.

EXERCISE

When you read any book, including the Bible, imagine the setting. Try imagining the problems: When Moses drops the heavy tablets at the sight of the Golden Calf, do they fall and crush his sandaled feet? How can you supply a tasteful grouping for a circumcision? Arrange the room where Raskolnikov breaks the vase in *Crime and Punishment.*

Try envisioning book jackets, too. Do you read mysteries — detective stuff? What will express the dilemma, showing something relevant to the plot and the mood, without giving the ending away? And just as a cover helps sell the book, so a poster does for plays. Do a poster for HAMLET. Do another for a less well-known play. Again, the mood, the spirit, a hint of the content, all help attract an audience. I mention enlarging a sketch. Take a small photo or postcard and draw half-inch squares on it. On a large sheet draw three-inch squares. Transfer (enlarge) the small drawing.

CHAPTER TEN

Broadway Briefly

S OON AFTER ICEMAN, and a year before LONG DAY'S JOUR-
NEY, José was asked to direct a play on Broadway: Ted Apstein's
THE INNKEEPERS. This was José's first play on Broadway, and he
asked me to design it — my first as well.

The set was the courtyard of a Mexican inn, with a bedroom placed
to one side. I elevated the bedroom two steps to help separate it from the
courtyard. Borders (overhead masking cloths) were of leaves, and a heavy
wisteria vine ran up the courtyard wall to justify them. The essence of
the play was that the owners of the inn are fleeing — trying to solve their
troubles by running from town to town, owning one inn and then another. There was nothing in this that seemed to be reflected in the setting: we simply had two spaces in an attractive inn. It was the lighting that
underlined the drama of the couple's battles in the bedroom, and made the
courtyard either pleasant or sinister.

One problem was that the producer ran out of money before the set was
finished. It was built, but not fully painted. The lay-in was not quite dry
when it went into the truck. "Well," said Joey Tulano, the boss painter at
Rakeman's studio, "maybe better this than to dibble around with it."

Joey had only one working eye; the other had been lost when a tack flew
into it as a canvas was ripped off the floor. This was still the age of tack-
spitters. Do not try this. Do not take a mouthful of blue tacks and spin a
magnetic hammer in front of your mouth, removing a tack on each pass,
the tack facing the right way as you spin the hammer again and drive it in
with one tap, fixing the cloth to the frame or floor, each tack driven in less
than two seconds, spaced at four or five inches. (Spaced too far, the cloth

drop will scallop when it is painted and shrinks. Too close, and you might hear the cry, "Who's the sonabitch what every inch tacks?")

Joey had become chargeman when Chester Rakeman, who had two huge hearing aids but heard what he wanted to hear, was standing behind a drop and heard the former boss painter tell his crew to take it easy, they could all use some overtime. (Again, never talk behind a drop.)

When we set up THE INNKEEPERS in Philadelphia, I spent the next few days finishing the painting. Union rules forbid this. The set designer doesn't paint his own scenery; and a local union paint crew should have been called in. But we had no money. I was staying at a cheap hotel, at management expense, of course, and every night when I went there to sleep briefly, a note waited for me: "DAVID GO HOME." The prop man became sick, but phoned me from the hospital and, with what might have been his last breath, croaked, "Don't lay out your own money."

The steps to the bedroom were stingy because I needed every inch in the courtyard. Our wonderful Geraldine Page, not a complainer, had some difficulty. I suggested that she place her feet in a more sideways manner, but that was uncomfortable and we rebuilt the steps.

When lighted, the stage actually looked good. But there was more trouble: we had no theater reserved for us in New York. This was a time of a major "theater jam." Too many shows; not enough theaters to house them in New York. And even the theater we were playing in Philadelphia had another show scheduled and we had to relocate while we waited for a spot in New York. The only "interim booking" I've ever heard of in Philadelphia. So we moved down the street, set up, and lighted again. Then our producer arrived with the good news that we had secured a theater in New York. It was good until the next morning, when we read in the newspaper that our booking was the shortest in history: we would open on a Tuesday and have to move out Saturday night. Of course if we were a giant hit, things could be shuffled, but unless the reviews were raves, there was no chance of our audience growing over time, fueled by that famous publicist, "word of mouth."

So we went into New York and opened at the Golden on Forty-Fifth Street. Reviews were bad. We closed Saturday night.

WHAT I LEARNED

When I started the design of THE INNKEEPERS, I realized that all the work I had done was in prepared theaters that were already in use. Here, we were renting empty theaters and it was up to us to create what happened downstage in the first two feet behind the proscenium, where the asbestos curtain, the house border, the house curtain, the inner-stage portal, and the first pipe and booms of lights must live. In that order. I went to Jo Mielziner and he showed me what to do. We became friends, and twenty years later his ashes stood on my piano for a week.

I met Jo because my father knew Richard Rodgers from college, and had taken me to see him. Mr. Rodgers's Connecticut home was beautiful, but somehow I had stepped in dog shit on the way in. I noticed this gob sticking up from my shoe when I sat down in a comfortable armchair and crossed my leg. An omen, predicting the rigors of the first musical I would designed for Mr. Rodgers. And I forgot what Roger Furse would have boldly and appropriately exclaimed: "Yech, dog shit!" I just sat there.

That's all I remember about the brief, awkward meeting, except that Mr. Rodgers suggested that I meet his designer, Jo. He would send a message introducing us.

Jo lived and worked in the great Dakota apartment building on West Seventy-Second Street, where John Lennon was later shot. Jo's apartment was above the Romanesque arch of the entry, and his studio was on the right side of the courtyard. It had two workrooms, one for Jo and a larger one for his assistants. We liked each other immediately, and he suggested I might work for him when not designing on my own.

I also learned about kickbacks while working on THE INNKEEPERS. As my damp, unfinished scenery was being loaded into the trucks, bound for Philadelphia, Chester Rakeman handed me an envelope. There was a hundred dollar bill inside, a lot of money then. I asked Ray Sovey what that was all about, and he said that it was common practice, that Chester wanted to build my next show. I gave the money back and did not participate in kickbacks — although once I asked a prop shop to help me finish a table for my home, and I'm ashamed of that.

When we rebuilt the steps to the bedroom, the producer asked me how much it would cost, and I guessed too little, which placed our carpenter, Joe Harbuck, in an awkward position. He gave me a dressing down: "My job, not yours."

Darren McGavin, the show's co-star, took me aside after I gave Geraldine the failed lesson on step climbing. He said he had once been a designer, and cautioned me to be careful of defending your scenery — it makes you look like a sore loser. A good lesson. I sometimes remembered it when I was defending my scenery.

I had been smart enough to say to the producer, as we drifted in Philadelphia, that the set would fit into any theater in New York except the tiny Golden. As bad luck would have it, that was the theater chosen for us. I reminded the producer of my warning, and he said, "Tough shit, that's where we're going. Stuff it in." I said I would, but it wouldn't look so good. "Would it look better in the dump?" he asked. So Joe Harbuck stuffed it in, and it looked okay from most seats during its brief pause on Broadway on its way to the dump.

By that time, everyone was mad at the producer and said they would not go to his opening night party. In support of them, I did not go. They all went. I learned: go to parties.

There was, and probably still is, something called "balancing." This means that you are doing two shows at once, and use money from one to help out the other. Each show is a separate corporation and this is a felony. Our producer was mounting another show at the same time, so perhaps we ran out of money because it was syphoned off.

I joined the crowd of newly arrived designers who visited producers with their portfolios. We were usually welcomed. It was relaxing for most producers to sit for ten minutes and look at pretty sketches of sets or costumes. And, who knew, a good idea might lurk in these displays. Herman Shumlin's dog chewed up one of my drawings, and to this day I dislike Cairn Terriers. But the response was always the same: "When you do a play on Broadway, I'll go to see it." Now I'd done such a play, and the response was either "Well, it flopped," or "I didn't see it for the few minutes it was in town." (By the way, drama producers rarely see dance, and dance people don't often go to theatre. Opera is yet another island. Something to keep in mind as you pitch your sets across genres.)

THE INNKEEPERS was my first Broadway play, and I expected more work from it. But it failed, and there were no offers until LONG DAY'S JOURNEY INTO NIGHT came along the following year. That was a huge success and I was well reviewed, but, again, no offers. So I returned to painting the scenery of other designers. It seemed strange to me, and also I was concerned that I was "typed" as a gloom designer.

I learned from the flamboyant and varied failures in our production of THE INNKEEPERS that there was truth in a remark Boris Aronson made to me when I worked for him. He said (Russian accent important), "Every show has its *wictum*. Learn early who da wictum will be. Be not da wictum."

I learned to work with stage crews. Never show up early, because then you'll be seen as impatiently waiting for the crew to arrive. Be five minutes late. Don't be impatient during coffee breaks. Offer to get the coffee — not as the generous supplier, but as a messenger. And don't fall for the oft-heard complaint that stagehands are paid too much and they drive up ticket prices. Nonsense. There are abuses of the system, but not many. These workers are smart and skilled and devoted.

The matter of defending your scenery, mentioned by Darren McGavin, can be delicate and hurtful. Here is such an example. The play was THE GOODBYE PEOPLE, by Herb Gardner. Herb was a brilliant man, a playwright and cartoonist, but he should not have directed his own play, for the usual reason. The playwright (or any author) has trouble cutting his or her golden words, and the play ends up being too long. (I once asked designer Peter Larkin how he guessed that a script was to become a success. Peter raised his hand, palm up. "It's light," he said). THE GOODBYE PEOPLE was set on a beach, with tons of real sand downstage and the raised boardwalk upstage. A small refreshment stand was tucked under the boardwalk. By the second act, the stand's owners had decorated it with a surround of tropical palm trees. In the intermission, that foliage and the trees had flown in, surrounding the stand, and perched above it on the boardwalk. The point in the play was that it was freezing midwinter, no one was on the beach, and the tropical props were funny and foolish. Herb decided during our previews that the last major speech of the play should be delivered upstage center, on the boardwalk, and the foliage would have to be moved aside.

"Herb," I said, "the stage picture will look lousy, the stuff will have to be re-rigged, and then there won't be time or money to change it back if the actor's position doesn't work. Anyway, the top of the boardwalk stairs, over here, is better, isn't it?"

As on any show, we were working long hours under pressure, and had become tired and crabby. Herb wasn't just mad, he was enraged. "I'm having trouble restraining myself, David," he said — and I got ready for a punch. (That can happen — there are legends, one being that Herman Shumlin dislocated his hip by aiming a kick at the designer Howard Bay.) We made the change Herb wanted, it didn't work, the set was spoiled, and he eventually placed the actor at the top of the stairs. What did I learn? Try to make your suggestion without doing the director's work and redirecting his scene. Maybe I should have said, "Herb, that's going to spoil the very look that you asked for. Are you sure there's not another location for the speech, close by?" It probably wouldn't have worked, but it's worth suggesting in the safety of these pages.

As I mentioned, we work under great pressure. So do lawyers and others, but in many professions there are ways to delay, to get needed time. We rarely have those options in theatre. The curtain has to go up. Lesson: Try to not snap at each other. Count to ten (quickly if necessary). On the positive side, we understand this and forgive.

By now I had learned to apologize for my errors — and anyone else's within range. This is usually the best way to put bad things behind us.

EXERCISE

Golden advice: Never spoil a good apology with an explanation. Try this next time you apologize. Can you break the habit?

CHAPTER ELEVEN

The Exploding Chicken

THIS CONCERNS MAGIC, but magic without sleight-of-hand. My best example follows, occurring some years ahead of this moment in my narrative, but it shouldn't be put off longer.

I started and ran, for thirty years, the National Theatre of the Deaf. Wonderful actors using the beautiful language of signs, matched by well-spoken words of hearing actors onstage in the mix. This dual form of seen and heard language was perhaps the only innovative stage form in the last half of the twentieth century.

Our best full-length plays, UNDER MILK WOOD and KING OF HEARTS, were directed by J Ranelli. Among other special qualities in the latter play was our scenery. It was painted as we went along — yes, as the scenes progressed. During the performance, flats covered with white paper were delivered onstage to Chuck Baird, one of our finest actors and a clever painter. With quick decisive strokes, he created the asylum walls, the café, the great town clock — whatever was needed. But here is my example of magic: There is a moment in the play when the frightened members of the local asylum, now at liberty, look out over the town walls toward the battlefield. A bomb was needed. I didn't want to apply for fire permits in every town we played. Here is what we did. The stage manager, who had been toting out Chuck's bare flats, now pushed out a chicken on her nest. The chicken was a red balloon with a yellow paper crown for her crest and paper wings draped over her back. Suddenly the whistle of an incoming bomb is heard. The deaf actors didn't hear that, but they all spotted the bomb as it flew in, and in unison ten heads followed its course down to the chicken. A pin on the end of the push-pole was activated and — *bang!* — she exploded.

The crest and wings jumped; the actors jumped. It worked. The audience knew what happened, had known what was going to happen, and laughed at the clever and anticipated idea when it succeeded. It was a magical moment, nothing concealed, which was the essence of its quality.

Ranelli told me of another magical moment in a play, when a cowboy squats onstage and pulls out a paper fan from his back pocket. He spreads it and puts it on the floor in front of him. On it is painted a lively small fire. He warms his hands and, I suppose, makes his coffee over it.

At the opening of Sheridan's THE CRITIC, which we performed under Joe Layton's direction, the fort's morning gun sounds and the guards awake. Again, with deaf actors, what to do? Something simple and obvious: a cannonball flies out of the wings and bounces across the stage.

Another instance: There is a famous eavesdropping scene in THE THREE MUSKETEERS. Onstage is the iron stove, and its stovepipe carries the message from the other room. In our case, the eavesdroppers watched hands reaching out from the stove and "speaking."

I designed Samuel Beckett's ENDGAME off Broadway for Alan Schneider. There was a window painted on the bare brick back wall. Just a crude child's window, a square with crossed lines within it. But one corner was painted on a hinged aluminum strip and was lifted by the actor when he pretended to look out.

WHAT I LEARNED

Memories of these moments make me wonder: How much in this frantic world of comedy and tragedy is real? How much of my life, of all of our lively, interwoven threads of applause and failure and hope, has been a dream? I remember moments that were real: the moment I pushed my grandson Jordan, six years old, on his first bike ride without those extra wheels. For a moment, as he wobbled down the street and I raced after him, I understood why I was here, why my parents had been here, why this little boy was here.

Next I recall a moment in a new ballet, with dust in the stage air still suspended after a long day's work. The dust caught the blue downlight, and the dancers walked through this wall of light, magically materializing. It was a final effect so entrancing that when the curtain came in, two thousand people sat still, unable to applaud. Then the soft Russian accent at my shoulder: "David, is beautiful." That moment was real.

Standing with my son in the tiny cockpit of a small sailboat we had built, off Cape Horn, was real. If I'm lucky, the last words I will remember are my son's, calling from on deck: "Dad, I think I see the Horn."

The forty-six years with my beloved Leonora were often real — often enough. Or am I making that up? She was there at another real moment, at the end of a performance by the company of deaf actors. The curtain rose for the bows, and a dozen beautiful children ran down the aisles and onto the stage, arms full of flowers to give to the handsome performers. The city was Hiroshima.

Now I remember my daughter, six years old, dressed in a bright red skirt and white tights, sitting on the auditorium-to-stage bridge that spanned the orchestra pit at New York's City Center theater, looking down at the musicians as they rehearsed Mendelssohn's magnificent overture to A MIDSUMMER NIGHT'S DREAM.

How strange, how unreal, that so many of the moments in my life that I remember as real were formed by the search for illusions.

EXERCISE

Sit quietly and sort out the moments of magic in your own life. You are entering this world of illusions. The impact, the contrast with your "ordinary" life, may strengthen your ability to imagine.

CHAPTER TWELVE

Sir Tyrone

....

A PRESS AGENT used by Circle in the Square became a partner in producing Paddy Chayefsky's new play THE TENTH MAN, and asked for me. This was a happy production, and I'm proud of the setting. Garson Kanin (director of THE DIARY OF ANNE FRANK, FUNNY GIRL, and author of books like *Tracy and Hepburn*) was involved at first, but suggested Sir Tyrone Guthrie instead of himself as director. Sir Tyrone, he argued, would see THE TENTH MAN as a fable, not as a Jewish play. "Snow White and the Seven Dwarfs," someone named it. This suggestion was generous of Garson.

I would design this show and then Sir Tyrone's next three, his last New York productions. Clear in his desires, he was at every turn a delight. Tony — that's what he was called in production — was an imposing man, six-foot four or, as he said, one-point-ninety-three meters. People who have a shambling gait, like Tony, look taller. Our eyes assume that they'll straighten up and gain height.

We met on the lower East Side of New York. At that time (1958) storefront and parlor-floor synagogues were still in place and in use. For two days Tony and one of the producers and I toured these old-world rooms, often a brownstone floor-through. Some were simple; some had vestiges of the old stained glass or beautiful arks and reading stands brought from the old country. The sextons who let us in were generally about five feet tall and grumpy, reminding me of the German opera directors I met who had fled Hitler.

Tony dealt handsomely with the Yiddish we heard, making himself clear —"Just a glance, old chap." My memory is of the tall ruddy man striding (long strides) up and down the aisles, a handkerchief knotted at the corners and balanced on his head — a poor imitation of a yarmulke. The panicked sextons scampered behind him. One old synagogue had a pressed-tin ceiling that could add appropriate interest, even beauty, to the shabby but enchanted room we wanted onstage. "I want the stage deep," said Tony. "The men rarely leave it, but when not involved they should pray or sit in shadow far upstage. The action, the comedy, is downstage."

After these two days, Tony went home to Ireland and we corresponded. He was articulate and knew stagecraft. When I suggested high windows, he wrote that if they were deeply set we wouldn't need backings. Did he want graffiti on the brick wall that would back the entrance door to the room? "You mean 'John loves Mary'? Never mind. You only see it open for a second."

I had been struck by a skylight in the ceiling of one of the brownstones, and this could be a source of fantastic light during the sunset exorcism. Also, there is an earlier moment when God, or Godliness, enters the room. Could the entire ceiling glow with golden light? Tony liked the idea, and defended it when the producer questioned the extra cost. Our electrician and I worked out the careful concealment of strip lights above the gauze ceiling. When the cue came on in dress rehearsal at the Walnut in Philadelphia, the effect exceeded my hopes. "Congratulations, David," said Tony, and he said it loud enough for the producers to hear, but not as a trumpet call to suggest his primacy. He had a keen eye and earlier, in light rehearsals, he advised me to cut out my cool (blue-toned) lighting circuits. "Waste of time; it should all be golden," he said. "Okay, but I believe I need one in the rabbi's office," I said. "Right-o" was the answer.

A problem with the set, similar to the tight two-room set of THE INN-KEEPERS, was that the rabbi's office shared space with the main room of the synagogue. There wasn't room onstage for both to exist side by side. The solution was to place the main room on an eight inch platform. The small rabbi's office was not on this platform: the actors stepped down into it. In addition to the seven or eight feet assigned to this office, we cut a narrow notch downstage into the platform of the main room, stretching about five feet toward center. A low-backed sofa, five feet long, sat there.

The sofa was useful, and the main room, immediately upstage of it, lost no width.

Tony never hesitated to admit he was wrong and we all were urged on by his confidence that allowed the frank and easy apologies that lubricate any work. We adored Tony, cast and crew. He made practical sense. "Damn, Tony, I've got a dead spot by the door." "Carry on, David, it's not worth refocusing before New York. The actor only passes through it once, and quickly."

Philadelphia boasted the original Horn and Hardart automat. Charlie Bugbee, our electrician, was a Philadelphia boy, and we ate our lunches there, near the Walnut Street Theatre. One day, we heard a man near us say to his wife that he had seen our play and was ashamed at the poverty of the synagogue we portrayed. Another customer turned to him and said, "Nonsense! Our first synagogue here was at a converted gas station and we prayed by the pumps!"

We enjoyed the legends about Tony. They were lessons, too. For example, an actress once said to him, "Dr. Guthrie" (he did enjoy that title, bestowed, I believe, by Queen's University of Belfast), "Dr. Guthrie, this moment has no reality for me." "Young lady this is theatre, not reality — if you wish to observe reality, go outside and watch a street fight. Now press on!"

After this I designed three more plays for Tony. We designed the living room furniture for LOVE AND LIBEL in the style of automobiles of the period, with tail fins and chrome insets. You could find this overstuffed junk in stores, of course, but you must transform it for stage, and usually exaggerate a bit. One set I designed for ballet used tents and needed tough bright material. The best fabric? Tent material? No. Step back, and transform it.

I then designed DINNER AT EIGHT for Tony, and that worked well enough. An all-star cast. I forgot to ask the kindly Walter Pidgeon if Greer Garson was truly the most beautiful woman ever born. One aging star phoned me at home to make sure that I had included footlights in her scenes. I had. We all knew that some older women had contractual agreements demanding these flattering lights, which wash out bags, shadows, and wrinkles.

Tony and his wife, Judith, lived frugally when in the New World, and an invitation to their flat for dinner might involve not much more than a can of peas. One night during the New York previews of DINNER AT EIGHT, he invited my assistant John Gleason and me to a restaurant dinner. We were surprised and delighted. Just before dessert, after the most inexpensive dinners we could find on the menu, he said, "Now boys, you know that Judith and I devote our time at home, Annaghmakerrig in Ireland, to a cottage industry we have created. We have put eight women to full-time work making jam. I hope you will become investors. How about two hundred and fifty each?" "Yup," we gulped — and we did follow through.

Are these stories strange? Do we work closely with the great, the towering figures of our industry, and talk about canned peas and jam? Yes. Read more about Sir Tyrone on the Internet, or buy the fine book he wrote or those written about him. Johnny and I were proud participants in his jam industry.

WHAT I LEARNED

The British are masters of insult. Never try to outdo them. One trick Tony described to me, but happily didn't use — nor have I (yet) — is to accuse your opponent of exactly what you know he hates in you.

Learn your local idioms. On opening night of LOVE AND LIBEL, Tony made a mistake. We needed a few more minutes to get the curtain up, so he stepped through the curtain on to the forestage, said what was needed, and finally cheered the audience with, "Keep your pecker up." That's the way it sounded. The audience gasped. The word is *pecour*, an old French word for "courage." I can't find it in my dictionaries, but that's what Tony, red-faced, told us.

It is amazing how quickly mistakes are forgotten if they are recognized immediately — or at least early — and an apology, if needed, is swiftly delivered. I've said this before, but it is worth repeating.

Stay with the team. For GIDEON, Tony wanted a steep acting area, so steep that the actors struggled on it. The *New York Times* review, here inaccurately remembered, stated that the play was superb in all ways except for David Hays's set, so steep that the actors struggled on it. What to do? Write a letter? Ask Tony to write a letter? Absolutely not!

We needed dead bodies in GIDEON. These are hard props to put on-stage. The dummies we plan, build, and dress usually don't cut it. Why? One theory is simple: they are not acting. Do dead bodies have to act on-stage? Yes, strange as it sounds.

Similarly, dogs don't usually work onstage, however well trained. They may hit their marks and bark on cue, but they are not in the same con-tinuum as the actors. They do better in movies, and this is central to the difference between what is frozen on film and what you see, live, in the same room.

EXERCISE

Think of this: Do elephants "work" in AIDA? Better than dogs onstage, I believe. Why? They are like huge moving props, not pretending to act, not giving much of a damn about what is going on around them. Dogs are aware, that's their problem onstage. The best dog actor I ever saw was not Annie's Sandy, but one in a production I lighted, BABY WANT A KISS. He or she was a sheepdog of some breed, with a fur-covered face, and — perhaps the key — fur-covered eyes. Ponder this.

CHAPTER THIRTEEN

The Light That Failed

O N OPENING NIGHT OF GIDEON, a light failed to go on. And it was an important spotlight, on Fredric March, play- ing an angel of God. As the electrician was correcting the error, Paddy Chayefsky, the playwright, ran backstage to the switchboards and yelled, "That man is fired!"

Guthrie ran backstage also, but observed afterward, "Luckily I didn't arrive in time to do more damage."

I don't drink, but suddenly I thought it was time to begin. I headed across Forty-Fifth Street to a bar. Paddy rushed after me and grabbed my tuxedo lapels as we stood in the middle of the street. "You have ruined my play! You have ruined my play!"

"Uh," I answered.

"Ruined! Ruined! You!" said Paddy, and made a strange gurgling noise.

"So go write novels," I responded, meanly.

Paddy paused, sighed, put his arm around me, and bought me the drink.

Theatre is a venture involving many. Anyone, top to bottom, can wreck the result. Or improve it.

Years later, I met E. L. Doctorow at an embassy party in Tokyo. He had a translation of *Ragtime* coming out, and my company, playing in Tokyo, was invited. Someone knew that Doctorow was writing a play, so we were awkwardly introduced. I said that I was sorry a successful novelist would be put to the torture of our process, and mentioned Bill Gibson's remark that writing a play was like trying to paint a picture with colored mice. I also mentioned my churlish remark to Paddy Chayefsky. His reply, as I remember it, has weight: "Yes, David, point taken. I've been successful and can do things my way now. No one can bully me into making edits I don't want; I can reject a bad cover to a novel and so on. But I still have no control over how people read it. A paragraph at a time as they fall asleep? On the toilet? Jiggling on a subway ride? And if I ask if they got my joke on page forty-six, will they know what I'm talking about? With this play, I know I won't get the perfect cast or the costumes I want, I'll lose some rewriting battles, and so forth. But eventually the curtain will go up in front of a crowd that all came for one purpose, and they'll see the same thing at the same time. And I'll know if they got my joke."

A note about critics: Designers and all members of the production team will face them. Being behind the scenes does not protect us from scrutiny. Always remember that while you are doing your job, critics are also doing theirs, and *these are separate jobs.* True, critics could understand better who does what onstage, and how much a director like Sir Tyrone is responsible for a good performance by an actor (or designer). I do like a definition of critics relayed to me by author Joanne Greenberg (*I Never Promised You a Rose Garden*): "Critics hide in the hills during the great wars of the arts, and when the wars are over, they come down and shoot the survivors."

Critics have their good side as well. When I started the National Theatre of the Deaf, it was generally regarded as a freak show. Two well-known critics, Elliot Norton and Sam Hirsch, came to see our opening, praised us in print, and thus set us on firm ground, with ammunition to sell our tours. Mr. Norton, whom I later came to know, had this formula: guess what the playwright intends and judge the success of that effort. That, he said, should be the centerpiece of a review.

Brooks Atkinson had recently retired, but our publicist for the Theatre of the Deaf asked him to see us and give a comment that, although it would not be published in a newspaper, could be used in our advertisements. He did that, and the useful remark was printed on our posters.

My favorite critic after Brooks Atkinson retired was Edith Oliver of the *New Yorker*. She always outlined the plot and the playwright's intent, and that helped you to decide whether to see it or not. Her own opinions influenced but did not make your decision.

We all suffered from the ego of a certain *Times* critic, and plays worth a visit were instead smashed. Another critic, one of the best, used the efforts of designers to inject a moment of humor or wit into his column, so we often played the role of those weathermen on TV news who create a light moment. Alexander Woollcott used to say things like, "The scenery was beautiful but the actors got in front of it." Another critic — a good one — refused to see the Theatre of the Deaf when we played Broadway. He said to me that he could not give an unbiased opinion of handicapped people. I blasted this, telling him that it was unfair not to judge talented people who want to show that they are gifted and valuable in many areas, and he should give them a chance. He didn't agree.

One can learn from critics. They can have insights and express them beautifully. My favorite example of this is from Donald Malcolm's review of a production of OUR TOWN that I did with José at Circle in the Square. This ran in the *New Yorker* on April 11, 1959: "Its author, Thornton Wilder, is much like an acrobat who modestly declines to try anything as difficult as walking the tightwire and is content to simply dance along the same route on thin air."

WHAT I LEARNED

This is worth repeating: you do your job; the critics do theirs; and these are separate jobs.

Bad notices hurt a play, and they can hurt everyone as a group or as individuals, emotionally and professionally. There is no cure, but stay with the ship, don't cast blame, and as Tony often said, carry on.

Newspapers and television stations and magazines hire critics because the public wants to read commentary and be advised whether to attend or not. It is important that a critic be skilled as a writer. The media want that and can judge it. Whether the critic is a good judge of theatre is another and often-overlooked quality.

Note also that critics gave legitimacy to the National Theatre of the Deaf. If your work is good, on or off Broadway, the chances are that critics will push it along. You usually have no choice about whether to be reviewed anyway, so take the chance. Painful as some critics can be, there are worse things than a harsh review.

When we played in Hartford, one newspaper decided to ask a deaf person to write the review. Not a bad idea in principle, but being criticized by someone without knowledge of our profession did not do our production any favors. The deaf person's opinion would have been interesting as a companion piece to the regular critic's column.

The lesson from all of this is to be careful when criticizing something outside your expertise. I forgot all of this when years later I was asked to write a film critique for the *New York Times*. The movie was about a sea voyage, and yes, I had recently taken one with my son and we had written a successful book. In one sense I was qualified, but I was not a professional critic. I criticized the film in some ways; the *Times* rewrote my thoughts, highlighting the negative; the criticism hurt the film; and I am ashamed of what I did.

EXERCISE

You'll be critical, if not a critic, of what you see onstage. But try Elliot Norton's system, at least for design, which concerns us here. First, what was the designer's intent? Then — did it work?

CHAPTER FOURTEEN

"Gadg" and Getting Fired

L ET'S GO BACK IN TIME. After LONG DAY'S JOURNEY INTO
NIGHT, there was no flood of design work, but the play did
attract an agent for me, Dick Seff at MCA. When he went on
leave, the famous agent Audrey Wood took his place. She suggested that I design THE ROPE DANCERS by Morton Wishengrad, and
when LONG DAY'S JOURNEY went to Paris, she arranged for Leonora
and me to take a side trip to Stratford to meet Peter Hall, the director-
to-be. At our pleasant lunch he said I would design the play — but somehow I did not. A year later, I worked for the producer, Roger Stevens, and
asked what had happened. "Audrey sold me the play and playwright," he
said, "then the director, then the two stars"— Siobhan McKenna and Art
Carney —"then two featured players. Then I said, 'Enough, Audrey.' I
guess you were below that cutoff, David."

The lesson here is simply financial: agents place their clients in descend-
ing order, starting with those who are paid the most and thus generate the
largest commissions.

Leonora and I went to see this play, and before curtain an announcement was made that Art Carney was ill, and his place was being taken by
his understudy, name mumbled. Ticket costs would be refunded. I said
that we could leave, but Leonora said that we would damn well not go,
we're in this game. The curtain went up, and there was a friend, Joe Julian,
in the role! We went backstage afterward, and I've rarely seen a man more
grateful. "It happened so fast I couldn't call agents or producers or friends.
You're the only people who saw me!" (By "people" he meant theatre professionals. Civilians didn't count.)

Then the play THE NIGHT CIRCUS, by Mike Gazzo, came my way. The fabled king of directors, Elia Kazan, had asked for me, possibly because of the success of THE TENTH MAN. At that time, Kazan was nicknamed "Gadg" (though soon he asked all to drop that and call him Elia). He was unpopular, even despised, because of his cooperation with Senator Joseph McCarthy. The general opinion was that he threw in names of possible communist-leaners not from any sense of moral responsibility, but because he wanted to continue working. I knew fine actors and directors who simply did not get phone calls for several years. No accusations, no open hearings — they simply were not called. I'd been too young for all of that, but friends not much older had been affected. One of these men had a purple heart from World War II, but he had been born in Russia. He came to this country at the age of six, and his older brother spoke Russian. Did I have a moral position here? I called him and others on the blacklist (or graylist) and asked for their advice or at least their prejudices. Work, they all said. You'll help no one by "taking a position," it's too late. And you'll learn from him. So I worked, and I learned.

Gadg came to my place and stretched out on the floor. He had an exceptional presence, not glowingly quiet like Balanchine's or large and forward moving like Tyrone Guthrie, but a crackling energy and a smile, a real smile that swept you in. From the floor, he said that he thought best when horizontal.

"What I want in NIGHT CIRCUS," he said, "is for the front door of the apartment to be downstage, way downstage. The bedroom can take the space it needs on one side and the door to the bathroom is on the other side. When the husband unexpectedly comes home, she is just coming out of the can; her lover is in the bedroom, and the husband is at the door, dividing them — they cannot get together in the fight.

He was so clear. I repeat his famous remark, "It's hard, but not complicated." Some directors have a gift of explaining with clarity, and others do not. When I was designing LONG DAY'S JOURNEY, José said that he wanted the room to have that feeling of Victorian light, which seems to hover in the room, suspended above the floor but not reaching the ceiling. I was not the lighting designer, but this was a useful image when I was coloring the room. Here's another image: "I want warm, wheat-colored light." Simple but not useful. "Warm" was vague but okay, but the wheat image blurred it for me.

Three difficulties about THE NIGHT CIRCUS: First, Gadg quit. The story I heard was that someone at a party said to him that it was just up his alley, that he could do it with both hands tied behind his back. He realized this was true and not the way he wanted to work.

The second problem with THE NIGHT CIRCUS was that it didn't turn out well. Frank Corsaro, a bright director who later found his métier in opera, took over. He ran the rehearsals in the improvised "do what you feel" style usually assigned to the Actors Studio and actors like James Dean. Al Lewis, playing the bartender, came onstage long before curtain and polished the bar glasses. "It's about doing and rehearsing, not just *feeling*," he said. "These 'method' actors think playing a role is as easy as going to the toilet. The result is the same — shit."

A third problem, certainly for me, was that I was fired from the lighting job. The dress rehearsal was poor for many reasons, one of those being that I did not have enough light on the actors. Something had to be done quickly, and I became the instant "wictum," given no time to fix the problem. I went to Audrey Wood, still my agent, for advice. It turned out that she was the playwright's agent as well. She never looked up at me from the papers on her desk. The playwright, her more important client by far, was fuming somewhere, "You can't hear my words if you can't see their faces. If you can't see their faces, you can't hear the words."

Now this is true; yes, it is. Interestingly, and not in my defense, the minimum light we need to see faces clearly has increased over 50 percent since the sixties. Sound levels have increased even more — at the levels we used in the sixties, we now feel we don't hear anything. In those days, plays and musicals were not artificially amplified. Now musicals, and sometimes even plays, are boosted. The electronic pickup can feed the sound through various filters, and the hollow sound applied to musicals keeps me away from the albums. Thank goodness the old standard still applies to opera. Learn to speak and sing out loud.

Another lighting designer was hired for THE NIGHT CIRCUS, and he responded by heaving bright light onstage willy-nilly. The result resembled a police line-up, and my set was ruined, but you heard the playwright's words — surely why the play closed so quickly. Another trick of this designer was to show off by loudly announcing his expertise while setting his levels. (They were all near full anyway.) For example, over the intercom, loudly, so that the producers could hear, "Joey, now with your left hand bring up dimmer three to nine, and with your right knee knock out dimmer four." I'm not complaining, mind you — this is wailing.

Shelly Winters was a friend to this production. She had been in Mike Gazzo's previous play, the successful A HATFUL OF RAIN. Now another work was being planned. I cannot remember its name, and it was never produced. Shelly asked me to lunch and described in detail all the furniture and knickknacks of her Brooklyn childhood home. All of them. Porcelain groups of plates announcing "Atlantic City," lamps with pink satin shades and fringes. "This could be useful in this new play," she said. "And if you forget any of this, phone my psychiatrist — here's his number — he has it all written down."

Lastly, the theater finally assigned was, once more, the beautiful but tiny John Golden. I said to the producer that I could *almost* jam in the set, but you know the rest of the dialogue.

WHAT I LEARNED

There was some illness in the cast of this play, not serious, and we continued on. This brings to mind Leonora's description of one of her tours, when she was dancing in the tenth-year road company of OKLAHOMA. The heroes of theatre are not the people who simply get out there without complaint and do their job at every performance, she said. The heroes are those who are subject to frequent personal injury and have a large family of loved ones, including pets, who are constantly on their deathbeds. But the show must go on, and the star's hysterical blubbering stops just in time for her to stride onstage from the wardrobe mistress's tender embrace. Heroism! Management is enthralled at this kind of courage and commitment.

I also learned from these "sink pissers" (the toilet is down the hall) that if every night you go to a different restaurant in a group and say you're celebrating someone's birthday, you might get a free dessert. This of course was a step up from the old days, when touring companies paid for your cheap hotel room and gave you meal tickets to a local diner instead of salary, and free dessert was never on offer.

Leonora also remembered a notable exchange. At one intermission the stage manager crossed from his position stage left to the switchboards stage right. "Larry, what happened to cues four and five?" "Sorry," was the reply. "I was busy putting out the fire."

Note the terms "stage right" and "stage left." This is the right and left of an actor or anyone standing onstage facing the audience. This is mildly annoying, and workers who've been onstage for years (me, for example), often give a little twitch of their right or left hand before heading in some direction. If you look carefully you might see this. Imagine the difficulty in England, where we say "prompt side" or "opposite prompt"— the problem being that the prompter might be on either side. In France we say "*au palais*" or "*au jardin*," the bulky palace being audience left and the gentler garden audience right. This follows the natural eye swing of a right-handed left-to-right–reading person.

When I was fired after the dress rehearsal of NIGHT CIRCUS, I remembered George Lord's admonition: "Never show a fool an unfinished work." The lighting was unfinished, yes — but so was everything else. Ordinarily I could have asked for more time, only an hour, to improve the work, but at that moment the playwright was distressed at the first appearance of his play onstage and a "wictum" was needed, and this is understandable. No one was a fool in this case; bad things simply happen. Or perhaps I was the fool: I should have lathered on more light at first and then nibbled away at it in subsequent rehearsals.

EXERCISE

In her novel *The Member of the Wedding,* Carson McCullers notes, "It was the hour when the shapes in the kitchen darkened and voices bloomed." Is this meaningful to you? Voice plus light plus seeing the speaker's face? You might even ask a friend to read lines as you experiment with lighting levels. How does the light affect the sound and clarity of the words?

CHAPTER FIFTEEN

Designing for Garson Kanin, and What It's All About

WHAT AN INTERESTING MAN, Garson Kanin. Playwright, director, author — a success at each, and generous as well. You may recall that he had given up Paddy Chayefsky's THE TENTH MAN to Tyrone Guthrie.

SUNDAY IN NEW YORK by Norman Krasna was one of Robert Redford's first Broadway plays. The play happened in a variety of New York City locales: a living room, a restaurant, a street corner. Garson's initial thought was intriguing. We were sitting in his living room and he said, "David, what troubles me is that a group reading a play can be excited and having a joyful time, but when the thing — particularly a comedy — hits the stage, with costumes and sets and rehearsed movement, it often stiffens. There is something lost, and it may be that initial fun of free-wheeling imagination, when you giggle and stumble and the lines are fresh. I wish this play could just take place in a living room like this."

"Let's try that," I said. The play does indeed start in an ordinary living room. Then we go to a Chinese restaurant. All of Norman Krasna's plays inhabit a Chinese restaurant at one point, Gar told me. "But," I said, "if it's a Japanese restaurant, all they have to do is sit on the floor."

"Yes!" said Gar, "and when they do, a woman in a kimono will come in, kneel next to them, and whip out an order pad from her sleeve."

And that's what we did, and it worked. The notion of sitting on the floor set it up; the waitress in kimono sealed it.

Do you remember those ugly pole lights? Three bullet-shaped light covers were mounted on a floor-to-ceiling pole, and you could slide them up or down and aim them. We used one in SUNDAY IN NEW YORK, making one light red, one yellow, and one green. This was not noticed during the first two scenes. But after the restaurant, everyone stood up; the red, yellow, and green lights glowed in sequence; and we were on a street corner. A small bit of action — looking at the light, someone putting out a restraining arm — again sealed the location. Magic without sleight-of-hand.

Another device we used created a rainstorm. We made a "rain curtain" from lengths of dyed blue clothesline, spaced about five inches apart. At the bottom of each line was a teardrop-shaped fishing weight. These weights at the bottom of each line were at different heights, and the result was a clear reference to those Japanese prints showing streaks of rain. It was zany, yes, and not exactly in the same style as the floor-sitting and the pole light. It was not part of the varied living room, having to fly in, but it carried a Japanese quality that matched the restaurant, and by this point in the play, zany extra effects were unquestioned. Or, as we say, it worked. Things that just "work" are not always explainable.

We isolated these scenes downstage as much as possible, often with side light that didn't spill upstage onto the living room sofa, which remained throughout.

Gar was fussy about props. There was a moment in this play when an actor playing an airline pilot packed his overnight bag, one of those small black bags on wheels that you first saw towed by pilots in airports. Gar thought that he should throw in a snack — a banana. The prop man supplied one, but Gar wasn't quite satisfied. At the end of our week out of town, in Toronto, after thirty-seven different bananas (according to our harassed prop man), the right size and shape banana was found. This thirty-eighth banana got a big laugh. Bigger than for the thirty-seventh banana. Why? Bananas are indeed called "the funny fruit," figure it out. But the thirty-eighth? Maybe the pilot threw it in the bag the best way.

Laughs are hard work. There was a costume sequence that gave us a big laugh in THE TENTH MAN. An old man totters into the synagogue. It is bitter winter. He starts, shakily, to take off his outer clothes. A jacket, a sweater, a sweatshirt. Suddenly he is down to a blazingly inappropriate orange football jersey. A laugh that was louder and longer than if he had simply taken off one jacket or overcoat. It was a finale to a process, a build-up of a pattern: one ordinary garment taken off while other things are happening onstage, then another, then another — a pause, the audience's attention wanders, then the sudden surprise. The skill of the actor was crucial to this success. Gauging how slow, how fast, garment by garment; at what moments to be shaky, to let a zipper snag, and so forth. The bit could have gone on for ten minutes.

It is said that comedy is more difficult than tragedy, and I agree. (It is also said that the messenger of tragedy is sound, while comedy is the province of the eye.) Once when I was at a lunch with William Gibson (THE MIRACLE WORKER and other plays) and Neil Simon, I was surprised at the deference given to Mr. Gibson by Mr. Simon. The serious, tragic stuff by Bill? Important! The foolish and superficial comedy by Neil? Well, many readers will not remember the good name of William Gibson; far more will remember the good name of Neil Simon.

SUNDAY IN NEW YORK was fun and a moderate success. I designed a second play for Gar, WE HAVE ALWAYS LIVED IN THE CASTLE, which did not succeed. Gar's rehearsal technique, as I saw it in both shows, was unusual. Actors arrived at the first rehearsal with their lines, if not yet memorized, well in mind. There was a full run-through. Then notes — excellent notes, appropriate for a first rehearsal. That afternoon, a repeat of the run-through, then more good notes. So it went, and lines were memorized by the second day's run-throughs, followed by two run-throughs a day, every day, right up to opening. Gar conducted his rehearsals from the seat of the *New York Times* critic. The most important seat, he said. It was up to the stage manager and me to race around the auditorium and seek out blocked sight lines and so forth.

My third encounter with Gar taught me a painful lesson. He had written a play and was to direct it. He knew I couldn't design it because of a schedule conflict. "But," he said to me, "come on over and talk it through with me. I'm eager to hear your thoughts, old friend."

He had already hired one of our finest designers and I knew that, but drawn by our friendship, I consented. This was a professional blunder. I had no business butting in. Also, secret meetings will become known.

Jim Hammerstein was the producer and we were a comfortable trio at Gar's house. Gar explained the plot scene by scene and I had an idea right at that moment. I explained it and said offhandedly that this would be a good help to the third scene. Gar had given no sign of tension, but he exploded. "MY PLAY DOESN'T NEED HELP!!" Wow. I fled, Jim drove me home in silence.

In a few days we met and talked this over. His brilliant wife, Ruth Gordon, was there, and despite the difficulty of getting out a full sentence with her in the room, I explained. I said that I loved my work and could not do it if I didn't believe it was important. It's secondary to the playwright's words and to good acting (what isn't?), but that does not prevent an artist or craftsman from making his or her specialty a satisfying life's work (Joseph Campbell's "bliss"). When I said I could "help" the third scene, I did not mean that I would lift it out of the mire, in which it was not. I certainly should have said that I had an idea to *support* (not "help") the scene. Even "enhance" would have been better, but not much. Why not just "use"? I believe that a setting should support all parts of a play, and that's why producers have found over the years that scenery can be a good thing, even if it's expensive. Or is it only that audiences generally prefer it because it's a tradition? We can do a play without scenery, in so-called black drapes. But that black void *is* scenery. It is a powerful statement about how you want the play to be perceived. This is often misunderstood.

Why not make the strongest statement about costumes by having none, the actors appearing nude? Whatever you take away, something is left. Anything placed onstage, I said to Gar, helps or hurts. I said that I did not accept the middle position of many producers that scenery is needed but doesn't do much one way or another. What professional in any field could endure that thought without losing pride and desire? Gar understood and agreed.

When the curtain goes up, you see a location or a mood — with luck both. Perhaps, as Robert Edmond Jones said, you see something that tells you what you will be experiencing. Is it just a room? Ah! It's set up for a children's birthday party. Does it imply impending joy or a start on the road to disaster? The design might suggest immediately which way it will go. Maybe the cards should be dealt out more slowly. My own LONG DAY'S JOURNEY INTO NIGHT began with a cheerful morning, but in a room not well kept. Surely anyone who paid the ticket price already knew that the family was cursed. The title suggests, even insists, upon the journey of mood to come. You see that everything can count: the title, your knowledge of the playwright's strengths, the actors' ranges, on and on. The designer has a thoughtful role to play in setting this mood. (There's that word — the "setting;" again, Robert Edmond Jones's label of the designer as "artist of occasions.")

WHAT I LEARNED

Do not do what I did with Gar: do not get between anyone and his or her work. But also, choose your words carefully. Remember too my dust-up with Herb Gardner.

Be proud of your work, and your contribution, or do something else. Stage design is not a secure profession, and if you don't have that theatre gene, you can go to safer work outside of our "floating world." The problem is that the theatre gene means you have the desire, but it doesn't guarantee skill or success. Many I've known have used up their lives in yearning.

Figure out how to add to the overall production, no matter how basic the setting is supposed to be. I remember two plays I set in dull apartments — and my settings were dull. Useful, yes. The doors were in the right places, so was the furniture. The lighting was bright enough. I didn't add much. But I think of what a wonderful designer like Peter Larkin might have done. He could take a dreary room, project the key message that the room was dreary, and at the same time give the audience something interesting to see. A plumbing pipe piercing a wall at a crazy place? Water damage? Obvious repairs or bad renovations that show a history and decline of the space? The point may be this: do not make the setting dull, but approach it as a space where you would not want to live. Perhaps the thought is that the space is inappropriate to the characters, not simply dull. A complex idea and process.

Some of us, like Peter, had special skills: Ben Edwards, for example, was brilliant with wallpaper (among his other great gifts), and his wall surfaces, though unobtrusive, were full of life.

The costume trick I noted tells us something about Sir Tyrone. At our first meeting, I asked him in what season the play took place, expecting the usual "It doesn't matter; make it easy; it's not important." But Tony said, "Midwinter. It's freezing; we'll have fun with coats and bundling up and zippers and all that." He was unafraid of what many directors would have regarded as annoying extra work, and he made it delightful.

EXERCISE

Write and then recite a speech to an imaginary high school graduating class. Be encouraging and be brief. Be clear. Three minutes.

··

CHAPTER SIXTEEN

The Pipe in the Drawer

··

ACTORS OBSERVE PEOPLE — and, of course, much else. As I've said before, the directors I've enjoyed most have been brilliant observers of everything. In college I studied art history: architecture, paintings, and sculpture. As I mentioned, once in Vienna I stood transfixed for two hours in front of a Bosch — and if I'd had the skill, I could have set up an easel and spent a month copying it. From the painting I learned a bit about the architecture of the time, but more about how people felt about heaven and the vividly depicted tortures of hell.

Designers observe things that reinforce what actors or dancers or singers are trying to do. Here's a simple example I used when I taught, an effort to start my students thinking: In De Sica's film *It Happened in the Park*, an exquisitely beautiful young woman and her father sit at a table, anxiously waiting. In the background, acrobats are rehearsing their flips, their springboard liftoffs, their landings on shoulders, and so on. We hear their grunts and see the strong rubber-bounce bodies in strenuous and graceful feats.

Another two people finally arrive, a homely young man and his mother. The father and mother talk, then argue — and we learn with distress that they are discussing the girl's dowry, and the woman is demanding a large sum. How can she demand so much when the girl is so beautiful and her son is a slob? Now the girl is in tears and stumbles to a fence by the table. The boy jumps up and runs to her. He says, kindly, "Please be patient. This is awful, but we will be happy." We realize that the girl has only one leg. My simple and obvious point was that the acrobats create a physical mood to emphasize the "problem" of the scene.

The things we can use are all around us, part of our lives. Here is another story I told in my classes. My father-in-law, Lew, was not a nice man. He didn't deserve affection from me or his badly treated daughter, my wife. He and his second wife lived in a dreary apartment overlooking a great confluence of roads in Queens, underlining the fact that they never went anywhere (contrast, contrast). They didn't serve tasty food or dish up interesting conversation. Their sofa and armchair remained just as they had been delivered from the department store, covered with a placenta of plastic, as if waiting patiently to be born, to emerge into real use, perhaps in a better world or apartment. That's a good scenic idea for a play. Lew's wife, Nettie, said her hobby was raising African violets. She had two small plastic pots of them on the windowsill, with little sticks announcing their prices ($1.25) still projecting from the bits of earth. But what was even more pathetic — and this moment still gives me pain — was when Lew noticed that I smoked a pipe. "I have one you can have," he said. "Haven't seen it for maybe ten years. I think it's in here." He yanked open a drawer in a kneehole desk and there it was, the only item in the deep drawer. How sad, how barren. Not an easy image to show onstage, but in a film a cleverly roving camera might catch the notion. Anyway, thoughts like this lead to other thoughts.

Students often asked what I preferred to design: plays, musicals, dance, or opera. (No one asked about the brassiere commercial I set in my early days.) My answer was that the joy really was in working with the director or choreographer. It's not about genre or complexity. Even what seems to be the simplest play can have challenges. Again, satisfaction is found in the support you ultimately bring to the production, whatever type it is.

I sometimes spoke in class about *The Lonely Passion of Judith Hearne,* a novel by Brian Moore that was to be dramatized. I was hired, but the play was never produced. The title character, Judith Hearne, is a drinker. She would be evicted again and again from the cheap digs she rented in Dublin. These tacky rooms are easy in concept, if not so easy to execute. Dull rooms? Again, not necessarily. We know rooms like this: just big enough for an iron-frame single bed, a bureau with a doily, and a washstand with its pitcher and towel rack. The toilet would be down the hall. A difficulty here is stretching out a ten-foot room to fill a thirty-six-foot proscenium — and I can't explain how; you just fiddle and fiddle and do it. (Imagine the small garret room in LA BOHÈME on a ninety-foot outdoor opera stage.) But it's not a real room; it's still scenery no matter how realistically you design it, and the audience will go along with you. There are many other things to consider in creating this "simple" space. Perhaps for Ms. Hearn, there would be a coat rack or some hooks on the door. A small wall mirror. A clothesline strung across part of the room to dry her underthings (her "smalls," the Brits might say). She probably had one cheap suitcase, and it would be stored under the bed. What to place on the bureau? When she arrived she would quickly unpack and place three or four items on it. They make any room her home. What were these few items she treasured? A photograph of her father? That seems better somehow than one of her mother. A high school graduation photo? Some sad, small piece of china, an imitation French porcelain, such as a shepherd piping to a lady or a sheep? Her own cross, to hang over the bed on a nail used for that for the past hundred years? Or was there a cross already there, part of the rental? If so, would she remove it and replace it with her own? Where would she put the displaced cross? And — most important — where is the tenderness here? These kinds of questions were fascinating to me, and one of my better actions would be to set up a good position (or two or three) for the actress as she unpacks and puts her objects in place. What about lighting? There is plenty to do with a bare-bulb effect, streaks from window blinds, or a candle she found in a drawer and lights to make a mood.

I had an experience relating to this. When my friend Charlie Bugbee's father died, I drove to Philadelphia to house-sit and field phone calls while Charlie and his wife, Virginia, were out making the arrangements. Charlie was a superb electrician and a friend — we did forty Broadway plays together. His father, also a gifted stage electrician, was a widower, and he was not a reader. What reading material was there in the house? I had my students imagine what they would include. This was in the mid-sixties. The old "if-you-were-on-a-desert-island" duo, a Bible and Shakespeare? I suppose there could have been a Bible, but I doubt the Shakespeare. The answer? There were two reading items — only two — and few of my students got this. One, obviously, was the *TV Guide*. The other was the last daily paper the father had bought. Today, perhaps an electronic device is all we might find.

WHAT I LEARNED

Look around. There's a lot in ordinary life, your daily life, supplying the dramatic contrast that counts onstage. Imagine scenes built from these observations. These images become part of you, part of your storeroom. In the film *All That Jazz*, the director's recurring dream takes him to a dusty, cobwebbed attic with many chests of drawers. He searches. He opens a drawer, looks in, closes it, goes to the next... on and on. How perfectly this describes my mind, and the minds of others like me.

What are the significant items in my own life's setting? I have a small porcelain piece, not a shepherd and lass, but a nude lady and a cat. She has a wanton yet innocent air. It was given to me by Roger Furse, my London teacher, and she is my muse. She would be the first thing I would rescue in a fire, after my wife, children, cats and dogs. Judith Hearn would surely treasure her few objects, and the way she unwraps each one, dusts it, looks at it, and places it can be revealing. I have a lot of material treasures, she has perhaps only one. She might take a long time with it. Think also of Laura's tiny figures in THE GLASS MENAGERIE. A vast collection? No, the very point Tennessee Williams wants to make is the pathos of the small, the treasured inadequate.

In a revival of Arthur Miller's DEATH OF A SALESMAN, at a moment of distress to Dustin Hoffman's character, his spectacles fall off. That small action precipitated a sudden loud sob from the entire audience. The spectacles were rimless, as I remember, and somewhat pretentious for Willy Loman, the salesman with worn heels (but also a shoeshine!). He is a man — a character — we care about, and the pretentious glasses lie at his feet as we feel his distress. I recall the debonair shoes worn by that man writhing in pain after his fall into the orchestra pit. In that case, I had no reason to care for that stranger — until I saw his shoes.

Observe and see contrasts. The small and everyday can be noticed or revealed to us, and then made by us into something big and powerful.

That's often what theatre is all about. Theatre, said my friend and co-worker Gene Lasko, is about compression. Things come together, then are torn open to make a drama. The compression is explosive, and a small spark can blow it up. Gene said that the day a play takes place is a special day. "Except Chekhov," he added.

EXERCISE

What do your treasured objects (objects, not people) mean to you? How do you, or how would you, protect them? You might even photograph (or draw) these objects in their current settings. Then study the photographs. What do you see? What would you include if you were to set these items in a production?

CHAPTER SEVENTEEN

Maureen and More

T HE CRITIC CLIVE BARNES said to me that a critic generally knows, when the curtain is barely halfway up, whether the play will be a success. "You just sense it," he said. "A lot to do with the designer's work." But these expectations can be cruel. I designed Neil Simon's THE GINGERBREAD LADY, and it was not his usual comedy, but a serious and well-written drama. No one got it. Where were the laughs? You can't always break those chains.

The play was set in a city house floor-through, and the producer, Arnold Saint Subber, suggested that we do away with the usual couch. "She's a drinker; why not scatter a few small tables and chairs around, as you would find in a bar?" This was done. When the curtain rose, no one in the audience said, "Ah, she's a drinker." But as the play proceeded, Maureen Stapleton moved restlessly from table to table, as if she were looking for a drink. This furniture did not by itself identify her as a barfly, but it gave her some tools to help create the character.

By the time I worked on this play, I had developed a helpful system of designing. Too often a director will be seduced by the rendering, cowed by a pretty sketch that is ready to be framed and exhibited. But then when the set is onstage, it doesn't work. Instead of this, I would conceive the set in my mind, or from rough sketches, but show up at the director's home or office with a blank drawing pad and a soft pencil. We'd sit down, and I'd place the pad on my knees and say, "Okay, let's put the desk over here." And I'd sketch it. Then, "The front door can be here," and I'd sketch that. As we went along, the director might say, "No, a bit more left," and so forth. Then I'd go home and do as nice a sketch or model as I could. I'd show it again to the director, and then to the producer. This process is quite different from not showing a fool an unfinished work.

I was privileged to have other encounters with Ms. Stapleton. I spent thirty years enthusiastically raising money for the National Theatre of the Deaf, and we would often have fund-raising parties ("benefits"), with a star featured to pep up the invitations. Julie Harris, Jason Robards, Colleen Dewhurst, Hume Cronyn, Jessica Tandy, Zoe Caldwell, Mary Martin, Helen Hayes, Chita Rivera, Jacques d'Amboise, Max Showalter, Peter Walker, and Lee Remick joined us and helped. Maureen Stapleton participated one year. At her party, in an elegant Central Park West penthouse, the hostess didn't control her young children. While I was speaking in front of the fireplace, those rotten show-off kids were doing gymnastics at my feet. I could barely concentrate, and I feared that Maureen, nervous enough most of the time, without amateur acrobats, would flee. But at the back of the room, Leonora had her in a grip of iron. When she did speak, her plea for funds was calm and brilliant. "Mo, how'd you do that?" I asked. "David, up there you were thinking theatre. I was thinking nightclub."

Another play, A THOUSAND CLOWNS, was by Herb Gardner. Our brief dust-up at the end of THE GOODBYE PEOPLE was forgotten. Now Jason Robards was starring and Fred Coe was the producer. A familiar team. But I didn't design the play. I offered a thought, and I believe Herb resented it. The play takes place in a messy bachelor apartment, but one scene took us to a brother's more elegant office, where there was one joke: the phone is tossed into the wastebasket and Jason's voice comes tinnily from there. It was funny.

But, years before, when I was being taken to Broadway by my parents, I saw THE LATE GEORGE APLEY, designed by my future teacher and friend Don Oenslager. At the end of what was basically a one-set show in a pleasant living room, the curtain came in, and, after a brief pause, went out on a club room. Seated in comfortable leather armchairs, two men discussed the life of the deceased man. Even at that young age, I was uneasy about the shift and intrusion, a sudden caboose hooked onto the scenic unity of the play. The information conveyed in this tag-on might have been written into the scenes before.

Now I felt the same and stated it. To paraphrase my statement: "You know, the office scene is a one-joke scene. It seems to me to be out of balance to the physical progression of the play. An additional set for one joke is expensive to build, and to operate it, you'll need to pay three more stagehands. Surely there's a way to incorporate that good joke in the main set. Anyway," I said, digging my hole deeper, "if the show succeeds and you send it on the road, that's what's going to happen. So why not do it now?"

I never heard from my friends again about this play. The show was a success. I saw it, and I still thought the shift was awkward and unnecessary. When it toured after Broadway, the joke was incorporated into the main scenes and there was no office set.

WHAT I LEARNED

The people who stood by me when I raised money for the National Theatre of the Deaf were thoughtful and generous. Most theatre stars are, and I'm honored to mention their names. I now also have a higher opinion of the guts it takes to stand up in front of a nightclub crowd.

Your good idea can be badly received. State it anyway, but carefully.

Cy Feuer, a fine man and producer (GUYS AND DOLLS, ANNIE GET YOUR GUN, and more), had produced THE GOODBYE PEOPLE and smarted from Herb's inability to cut his own writing and from his own inability to control the situation. "Make cuts early," he said. "You don't have time to rehearse material you'll discard. The time spent on it is wasted and, worse, you steal from the time you need to rehearse the good stuff."

EXERCISE

See many shows. Don't just wait for the successes. There may be more to learn from the shows that don't work. Did their scenery help? Could it have? What went wrong?

CHAPTER EIGHTEEN

Good Things and Not-So-Good Things

I DESIGNED ALL THE WAY HOME, adapted by Tad Mosel from James Agee's *A Death in the Family*. Tad earned a Pulitzer for this play. Arthur Penn directed. The play was written with six settings, and Tad specified a turntable. There I did speak up, carefully, and was heard. One set could serve, I said. We could arrange chairs to make the Model T they take to visit grandma. Her home could be played downstage, in her backyard, and for that scene I would emphasize the trees that edge the set and it would look like the backwoods where the old lady lives. Much money and time was saved and no running crew was needed. As I noted, our final set was described precisely in Tad's stage directions when the play was published, and my students asked me what I had done that was so special — I had just followed the playwright's directions.

The problem was that the set had a somewhat romantic air, a home that seemed to float. Peter Feller built it. The designer Peter Larkin, whom I mentioned, sometimes worked for Feller Studios as a draftsman. That means that he took the designer's blueprints — or mere notions — and converted them into drawings that carpenters in the shop could read easily: perhaps a wall would be better understood if redrawn and seen from the back instead of the front. I had done this for Roger Furse in London. There was the placement of hinges, reinforcement for moldings, and so on. Peter said to me on this occasion, "David, drafting your stuff is like doing an engineering drawing of a fart." Fair enough.

A few things happened on the way to New York. We opened well in New Haven, but had to make a Monday night in Boston. The big set was taken down and loaded in trucks Saturday night in New Haven, and, with no sleep Saturday or Sunday nights, we finished the setup and lighting Monday night just before curtain. Fred Coe, an admirable man and our good producer, grabbed me at intermission. He was from Alligator, Mississippi, and when he was mad he talked just that way. "David, the only light you have onstage is reflected from the spectacles of the first-row audience."

"Well I told you we could barely set up and focus in the time you gave us."

"And I told you that the Theatre Guild wouldn't book us unless we gave all eight performances here."

"Instead of yelling at each other why don't we buy coffee and some take-out for the crew, who are three-quarters dead?"

"Good idea."

And we did that.

We argue in theatre. It's volatile work, done by volatile people, and no one minds much — and often the argument ends with humor. When my son and I voyaged together in a tiny boat, we practiced the "Big Rule," which states that if you're going to laugh at something six months from now, why not save time and laugh starting now?

I once used the big F-word over the phone to that exasperating man, producer David Merrick, and no one blamed me — not even Merrick, who soon hired me again. David had a pallor, and one designer said that he'd been tempted to punch him, but "It would be like putting my fist into a Roquefort cheese." Contrary to the beliefs of many he outmaneuvered, David had a saving sense of humor.

Concerning rough language, I felt sorry for my brother, doing brilliant medical research in an academic setting, where one mildly critical word, whispered, will never be forgotten. I was once asked to head an art department at a university, and I turned it down as too tough, with too much academic politics and infighting (because, as the saying goes, there's so little at stake). "But you've survived Broadway!" they said. I could only laugh.

Back to ALL THE WAY HOME in Boston. The day after opening, we had the usual notes for the actors, plus a focus touch-up, and finally notes for Ray Sovey and me. I had asked for Ray as costume designer, and his clothes were perfect. Again, I had gotten a job for one of my teachers! At one point in the play, Colleen Dewhurst and Lillian Gish sat on the same sofa. Arthur said, "David, I know you like Lillian, but this is Colleen's scene. Why is Lillian so much brighter? Colleen sits there in a black hole." When we set up the scene that afternoon, I fussed without results. Then Ray had the idea of asking the women to change places. Lillian still blazed; Colleen carried her black hole with her. "It's the makeup," said Ray. "Lillian is using old-fashioned grease paint, and look at that silent-film technique of tilting her chin up just a bit, to gather all the light she can. Colleen is using new matte stuff." Observations like that from an old-timer. Now I'm an old-timer.

Arthur was a meticulous and patient director, and he created a fine show. But some things cannot be controlled; they get away from you. Colleen was a powerfully realistic actor, and the initially wispy nature of her stage character, as we had envisioned it, didn't circulate in her blood. After we opened in New York, my friend and college classmate Stark Hesseltine phoned me. Stark had made a fine reputation early on as an agent. His tricks were to stay late at the office and keep talking to Hollywood, and also to thank people who auditioned his clients. Years later, when we auditioned twenty or thirty hearing actors in New York every year for the Theatre of the Deaf, I followed Stark's example and wrote thank-you notes to all the actors we did not hire. They were astonished at this almost unknown courtesy. Now Stark had a thought for me. "David, about last night. You know you blew it."

"Yeah, I know. Thanks. Keep it a secret."

In this case, Stark was saying the reason the set stood out (and was praised) was exactly because of the way it stood out. A nice-looking piece of work onstage, admired by many who did not grasp — or because the set did not grasp and support — the more realistic direction the play had taken. I thought of THE GLASS MENAGERIE, with Laurette Taylor lifting the play into a mixture of the real, the unreal, and the dream-memory of the real. There, Jo Mielziner's set of a real interior but with a dreamy, misty quality, was a bull's-eye.

We were all nominated for Tony Awards, and Colleen won hers as best actress. She deserved it. Whatever the disconnect, she always took the stage brilliantly. We were friends from Circle in the Square days, and Leonora and I spent time on her farm in South Salem, New York, where she had to lift cats out of the sink to draw a glass of water. One experience that Tony Award night revolved around Oliver Smith, who won his award in the musical category for CAMELOT. When they came to "best scenery for a dramatic play," only he and I were competing, and I assumed that he wouldn't win twice. I was halfway out of my seat as they opened the envelope and announced his name again, for BECKETT. What to do? Nothing, except to pretend I had hemorrhoids and sit down.

Arthur did not win that night. In the lobby on the way out of the Waldorf, he said to me, with some bitterness, that this could be a shitty profession — but he had a wonderful new project to look forward to. After THE MIRACLE WORKER, he and Anne Bancroft, who had played Anne Sullivan, had been approached by the government, the old Vocational Rehabilitation Administration. Would he and Anne start a theatre of deaf people, using beautiful sign language? Celebrities, such as athletes and actors, have always pulled minorities forward, and a theatre could do that. Deaf people, if they were seen as bright and talented, would advance and get better jobs, get off the dole and become taxpayers. "Join us?" said Arthur — and, of course, I did. But that thirty-five years is another story.

WHAT I LEARNED

When I was still in college, I met Lincoln Kirstein (I'll come to him). He sent me to meet Pavel Tchelitchew, and this artist said to me, the young student, that dreams are as good as realities. "Don't try to revive them, to make them come true again, because they *are* true. Let them be."

ALL THE WAY HOME was in three acts. Three-acts are rarely done today, and certainly this was last two-intermission play I designed. It was a poor choice for the National Theatre of the Deaf when we revived it (with Colleen's fine directing) twelve years later, because of those two intermissions. The audience thinned out remarkably during that second break. "Fled" might be the better verb. Not, I believe, because the play was badly done, but because of babysitters' schedules and our generally shorter attention span. The play had no consuming music as in opera or ballet. I should have asked Tad if we could try to rework it into a one-intermission play.

EXERCISE

You may be asked, or you may take it upon yourself, to suggest a rearrangement of a play or a multiscene musical. Read novels, decide what would make good sequences in a play, both literary and scenic. Is this your job? Yes, everything is your job. Read Kipling's *Captains Courageous*, then see the old film of the same title. This was a brilliant adaptation or dramatization.

CHAPTER NINETEEN

${HUGHIE,}$ and ${Strange}$ ${Behavior}$

O N A FRIDAY AFTERNOON, José phoned and said that he had the rights for O'Neill's HUGHIE, that Jason was available, and that we had to move fast. Rehearsals would start Monday, and we would be on for previews at the Royale in New York two weeks later. Then the business manager called. I said I'd do my damnedest, but I wanted one concession. Let us not lose two or three days by having a bid session and juggling competing bids. "Absolutely," was the answer. There were two fine shops in New York, Peter Feller's shop and Willy Nolan's. They were keen competitors but not unfriendly, and when Willy died a few years later, some of Pete's great spirit seemed to pass with him, and he soon retired. Willy was busier than Pete at that moment, and I asked that the show go directly to Pete.

I went to the Royale and measured. I designed the show, and showed José my idea and my sketch. All night Sunday, I did the working drawings for construction. The paint sketches could wait, since it was a simple paint job and could be described in words to establish its cost. On Monday morning, I gave the plans to our stage manager to set up the rehearsal stage. Then the business manager came in, grabbed them, and took them to another shop to compete with Peter. Two days wasted. The bid was $2,000 under Peter's and the other shop got the job. They put the show onstage quickly enough, but then the elevator didn't work. We spent over $7,000 in overtime dollars repairing it.

Fast as this process was for HUGHIE, news carries faster and a respected critic from a weekly magazine phoned. "David," he said, "I know how you should design this. Make the set small; a cramped space."

"Henry," I said, "we're going into the Royale and it has a forty-foot proscenium." (They are usually thirty-six feet for a smaller drama theater, as
opposed to a musical house.) "The Royale also has the widest backstage
on Forty-Fifth Street. I'm spreading out all the way on either side of the
proscenium opening. The set's going to be wall to wall, almost seventy
feet wide — and Jason will wander in it. I might not do this if the actor
weren't as strong as Jason. But he'll underline the cold loneliness of the
empty midnight space. I hope you like it."

"Me too," he said — and he did.

The set was based on the lobby of the Hudson Hotel, now demolished,
on Forty-Seventh Street. That was Damon Runyon's "street of dreams."
I spent hours in that lobby that weekend. The walls were a pale blue fake
marble, with square columns here and there, and a cage for the night clerk,
the one other character in the play, who listens to the monologue of Erie
Smith, Jason's character. There was another metal cage for the elevator, and
I put one small barred window upstage center. A dark blue line, five feet
up and an inch-and-a-half wide, traveled — relentlessly, I thought — across
the walls and the columns.

The set worked. When Jason called for the elevator, which contained
one bare light bulb, it cast spidery, scary shadows that raced across the walls
as the cage descended. Dawn could be seen through the small window.

The play was wonderful, Jason was magnificent, and we sold out our
previews. But Equity rules demanded that you cannot preview forever, so
we opened formally. The reviews were not all good, and we died.

After New York, the show was to go to San Francisco for a limited run.
But the old water cooler I had found, a unique and lively prop, was to be
left behind. "Too expensive to ship," I was told. That was nonsense. I got
the cost from UPS and it was reasonable. Jason, who wanted the prop, said
he'd share the cost with me. I went to the producer, not afraid to embarrass
him, and gave him the price. He explained that the price wasn't the real
reason. He'd promised the antique dealer that the valuable water cooler
would not leave New York. How sad. Why lie when the truth was simpler
and better? I asked the manager just that question. A shrug. These men
were not evil, just not devoted to the truth, and unable to resist tweaking
various expensive workers who "do not sell one more ticket."

HUGHIE was revived that summer in a small upstate theater. I was not involved, but Jason asked me to come up to see a matinee and have supper with him. My son, Dan, then fifteen, agreed to keep me company. The driving directions were confusing, I made mistakes, and we arrived late for the short play. Late indeed: as we were shown in, the last line was being spoken. Jason was on his knees with the night clerk, throwing the dice. "Easy when you got my luck — and know-how, huh, Charlie?" The dawn could be seen through the tiny window; the curtain came down. "Dad," said Dan, "you've finally taken me to a play that's the right length."

WHAT I LEARNED

One of the richest men in the industry, profiting legally by thousands of dollars each week, also pursued "ice," the profits made by selling tickets outside box-office bookkeeping. An insignificant tax cheat, but pure "emotional oxygen" for him. This always involves lying, but these are white lies to those who practice it: steps in a dance, part of a game, always with the delusion that nobody is hurt.

Malachy McCourt told me that a lie is just a wish you hope will come true. Or, as Charles Dickens puts it in *Barnaby Rudge*, "Not lying. Only a little management, a little diplomacy, a little — intriguing, that's the word."

Why do this? Why engage in nonsense like the story concerning the old water cooler? After that, I noticed that on my contract, a standard union form, someone had written in a clause above the signatures. It subtracted from my possibility to earn if the show succeeded. I went to the union lawyer with one of the producers, and the lawyer looked up and said, "In my forty years of union law, this is the first case of forgery I've ever handled."

"It's not forgery."

"OK, it's 'interlineation' or something, I'll just cross it out; initial here; thank you."

I often assumed I was given false information about my budgets, particularly the money I could spend renting furniture. If, that is, I even *knew* the false budget. It never seemed to matter. There was in Manhattan a huge and useful prop house — five vast floors of marvelous furniture from every period, plus fantastic pieces that fashion photographers used, like full-size leather elephants. You made your choices, but never knew what you were spending. "Don't worry, I'll work it out with your manager," said the boss. Figure it out.

These less-than-honest situations sprang up from time to time, as they do in all fields. In our rush from conception to opening, and the known risk of failure taken by participants, these tricks can be thought of as mere pranks, hurting no one. I mention this to describe one occasional aspect of our work, not to present my profession as a constant minefield of false speech and deceptive actions.

There are two mild and amusing reverse tricks. I never used them — I never had the chance. If you are doing, say, the living room of a shipping magnate, such as in DINNER AT EIGHT, why not furnish it appropriately with rare imports? Or at least with a symbol of these imports, such as Chinese Chippendale? Go to the prop dealers first and locate your furniture, *then* draw it in your sketch. Once the sketch is approved, you can take a hero's credit for having searched far and wide to locate the rare stuff.

A second trick, I'm sure common in other industries, is to pad your concept. If you know that any cost, no matter how low, will be disputed by a manager (knee-jerk negotiating), put stuff you don't need in your proposal. When the manager screams, just cut it out. Ben Edwards told me that he located a magnificent large vase for a set. "Too expensive," said the business manager. Ben found a less magnificent but cheaper vase. "Too expensive," cried the manager.

"So how much are you willing to spend?" asked Ben.

"*Nothing!*"

I'm proud of the good setting I did under pressure for HUGHIE. I never found a relationship between the quality of work I did and the difficulty of its conception or the speed demanded for conceiving and executing it. Some of my settings for dull plays were good, and happily the reverse was not often the case. I could have been pickier with which productions I worked on, as Boris Aronson claimed to be. But I followed directors, and some producers, and if José or Joe Layton or Elia Kazan or Robert Whitehead or Arthur Penn went into a play with little promise, I eagerly tagged along. I wanted work — I was not an ivory-tower artist, I was supporting a family. (Lincoln Kirstein called me an artist striving to be a craftsman, whatever that means.) But in the course of a hectic life, I produced some work that I'm proud of. The sketch for HUGHIE is one of three I now have hanging on my wall. I gave the only other sketch of HUGHIE to Jason. I also gave him a drawing that I found discarded in an alley outside a Washington, DC, theater. It was on white cardboard, with hand-printed dark-blue letters — a cue card to be held up for an actor to read. (This was before the teleprompters that roll the script across the camera lenses in television.) Probably from President Carter's preinauguration ceremony, it reads, "Good evening. My name is John Wayne."

EXERCISE

Read HUGHIE and then visualize the action in a cramped space, as the critic suggested. Then imagine it in a vast space. What are the strengths and weaknesses of each? What would be critical to each setting's success?

CHAPTER TWENTY

Two Designers and Survival

ARLY ON, Leonora and I met Pat Zipprodt, the costume designer, tall and handsome, with a lovely voice and large, beautiful hands. We had lunch. She soon became one of our dearest friends. The week after the lunch she phoned. "I hear you have an all-nighter coming at Circle in the Square."

"Yes."

"I'll be there," she said — and she was, and we worked through the night, and made it in time: sets, costumes, and lighting. That was THE QUARE FELLOW. Pat showed up at our place to visit one morning. I was sick, and went that day to the hospital for three months, with a persistent case of hepatitis. She moved in, helped Leonora with our children, and completed the work I had to abandon, while continuing her own.

Pat had a "little voice," which she had developed on her first job, driving around the Chicago suburbs with a one-woman puppet show, speaking for the puppets as they encouraged first-graders to brush their teeth. Every spring, on the first of May, the phone would ring, and there was the little voice reciting that Elizabethan poem: "The first of May, the first of May, outdoor fucking starts today." Then an even tinier voice: "Tee hee."

Here I cannot resist a story that illustrates how frantic our work could be and one way a designer wriggled out of a problem.

Pat phoned one afternoon after a long stay out of town, I believe with FIDDLER ON THE ROOF. "Eeg," she said (I was "Eagle;" I called her "Pin"), "is it true that we have to show up tonight and talk to [our next director]?"

"Yes," I said.

"Does he expect sketches?"

"Yes," I said, not mentioning that I also had not started.

"Eeg, tell me your impression of this play."

"Well, I believe it reflects the coming of the industrial revolution to France in . . ."

"Eeg! Who's in it?"

"Well, there's Napoleon . . ."

"Napoleon!? Who else?"

"The pope."

"The pope!? Which pope?"

"Napoleon's pope, but what does it matter, they all wore the same frock."

"Okay, who else?"

"A cardinal, a monk, and some soldiers."

"No women?"

"Oh yes, Josephine."

"Okay, see you there."

So that night the door was opened and we went into the director's apartment. Neither of us had sketches, but Pat was carrying a large brown paper bag, the kind of bag with handles and "Large Brown Paper Bag" printed on it. The young director was nervous — or, more accurately, terrified. This was his first Broadway show. Pat swept in; we sat down.

"My question," she started, and began to scoop out gallons of stuff from the bag, all white. There were swatches of white silk, white linen, white canvas, torn white paper plates, gobs of cotton, white lace, a tampon, on and on. "My question," she went on, scooping out more white tatters, "before we begin: I must know what you mean when you think of 'white'?"

The director's eyes were saucer-big. Broadway! The renowned Pat Zipprodt in his apartment! The basic questions of the universe! No more waiting on tables! Broadway! Conversations with angels!

And so it went. In an hour, we left the exhausted young man. We got on the elevator and the doors closed. "Tee Hee."

I must add that three days later she had read the play — all the way through — thought about it, and produced beautiful costume sketches.

There is another part of that tale. I designed the locales for this play and no one was pleased, including me. "Look at the poster," said the director and the producer. "Bold, dark space. Black velour, in fact, with a ramp or two." So against my better judgment I went that way. Not good; too bare. But I had included two magnificent paintings, jammed with colorful soldiers, horses, cannons. One showed Napoleon in triumph: Rene Theodore's scene of the surrender at Ulm. The other showed the dismal wintry retreat from Russia in 1812, painted by Victor Adam. These were reproduced in gigantic size, thirty-eight feet wide and twenty feet high. The first served as the show curtain when the audience entered. Napoleon's triumph could be eagerly studied by the audience as they waited for our play to start. The other was the curtain for Act II, setting the mood for Napoleon's defeat, and would be worth seeing during the intermission. A great effort, but the audience assumed they were part of the house furnishings, commissioned in olden times by the Shuberts and having nothing to do with this play. My contribution was seen only as the uninformative black surround revealed when these painted curtains went up.

Fred Voelpel is another designer to mention here. He had preceded me at Yale and at Green Mansions, and that summer I reused many of his scenic pieces and drops. (We painted over old drops.) But I didn't actually meet Fred until we designed NO STRINGS for Richard Rodgers. When I started the National Theatre of the Deaf, Fred came aboard for thirty years as our costume designer. He gave us good clothes, but much more. At the beginning of each producing process for each of the sixty shows he did for us, Fred sat down with the director I'd chosen and went through the show, character by character. Those directors feared Fred, and rightfully. "Who is this character, really? Why is he in the play? How did he get this way? What about his family? Where did he grow up? Are you going to give him a special gait? Facial hair?" On and on, and I saw strong men and women sweat during these meetings, as questions not yet considered came to the table. None of us wept; that came later. Fred could make the toughest wardrobe mistress weep. He was also the finest teacher of set and costume design that I ever met.

WHAT I LEARNED

I realized my luck in belonging to teams. Coming to New York, where the norm for designers is independent effort, I was taken in by Circle in the Square and José Quintero. Then I made alliances with directors: Arthur Penn, Tyrone Guthrie, Joe Layton, Elia Kazan. I became the designer for three seasons at the Shakespeare Theater in Stratford, Connecticut, then at the Vivian Beaumont at Lincoln Center, then the Metropolitan Opera's second company and, most intensely, with Balanchine at the New York City Ballet. Being a company designer gave me support and pleasure.

Now a sorry lesson. I discussed my failure in that play about Napoleon. Nothing drew the audience into the huge paintings with focus or energy as they entered the theater and settled themselves, or at intermission as they went to the restroom or chatted about things other than the play. This is an example of imbalance, another version of disconnect within an artistic structure, such as the extraneous set in THE LATE GEORGE APLEY. Something similar happened to a designer I knew who did settings for THE GIRL OF THE GOLDEN WEST, not Puccini's opera, but the original play by David Belasco. The sets were good enough. Someone had a respectable idea, to let us see the practice common when the play was written: a glorious sunset scene at the ending. And there it was: the final curtain came in and then out and there stood the couple, triumphant in the love that had lifted them above all difficulties, standing arm in arm on a mountaintop, and gazing upstage at the blazing heavenly display. A magnificent apotheosis.

Now visualize the scene in the auditorium. The designer is standing at the top of the aisle. The critics have shot out of their seats at the first curtain and are racing up the aisles to get to the phones or their offices and construct their reviews. "Turn around!" bellows the designer. "Please turn around! Look! Please look!" Now he's in tears. No one has turned, no critic has seen the beautiful effect in which talent and budget were invested. The audience, in no hurry to leap out of their seats, has turned around at the commotion, and too few of them see the glory. How to change this? Don't bring in the curtain before the effect. Dissolve in full sight from the last setting to this finale.

Designers are expected to do many things, to be at home in many milieus, to wear many hats. Mentioning Pat Zipprodt brings to mind her fine stage clothes for FIDDLER ON THE ROOF. Jerry Robbins, the director, was magnificent as a musical and dance director, but not so magnificent with verbal comments. There was the usual first meeting of the brilliant group that brought us this work. Authors, composer, designers and so forth. Jerry said, according to Pat, "It's hard to imagine anyone working on this production who isn't Jewish." All eyes swiveled to Pat, or away from her, the same signal. She said, "I thought of mentioning that I was the designer who did the clothes for MADAME BUTTERFLY at the Met, but instead I asked to be excused to make a phone call, and after a few moments came back into the room and said to Jerry that I'd just phoned my mother and yes, I *am* Jewish."

The designer for that production of FIDDLER, Boris Aronson, was denied a well-deserved Tony award because his settings "copied" (no, adapted) Marc Chagall's paintings. Besides suggesting that the judging panel was unaware of how complex our craft is, this attitude makes me wonder why the playwrights received awards, when their work was based on Sholem Aleichem's writing. For that matter, GUYS AND DOLLS was based on Damon Runyon's work; MY FAIR LADY adapted Shaw; and on and on.

Note that theatre costume designers prefer to call their output "clothes" instead of "costumes."

EXERCISE

Look at white. There are the actual tones which vary from a "dead white" to oyster white to milk white to bone white to eggshell and ivory and so forth. Subtle differences are emphasized by the surfaces: brilliant white canvas makes a far different presentation than the brilliant white fiberglass hull of a sailboat.

CHAPTER TWENTY-ONE

One Night Only

I DESIGNED A MURDERER AMONG US. Sam Wanamaker was the director. Tom Bosley starred and Fred Voelpel did the clothes. Working for Sam was delightful. He was already involved in his great work of creating a replica of the Globe Theatre in London.

This play was a pleasant but not strong comedy set in a small French village. I supplied an opening setting in a garret room, with walls rising about five feet and then slanting in to a small, flat ceiling with iron lacework around its rim and a chandelier hanging through a center hole. A small pedestal table sat center. Then we changed to the village square. The walls pivoted, and now the in-slanted ceilings became the out-slanted roofs of the houses surrounding the square. The garret room had been painted a plain off-white. We now saw the reverse side, painted with the doors and windows of the French village houses. The center ceiling was lowered to the stage floor and became the grassy village square, the iron edging becoming its border. One streetlight was at each of the four corners of the square; they had been atop the ceiling and not visible in the first scene. The hole in the ceiling was large enough to pass around the table, which remained. Just as the ceiling settled on the floor, the streetlights turned on, then after another beat, a small bottle sitting inconspicuously on the table squirted water — the town fountain. The timing had to be right: the process in exact order, timed the way an old-time stand-up comic times his jokes. A lot of fun, all that, and the people who saw it at the beautiful Morosco Theatre for its one performance were pleased with it. One performance! Bad enough that I had the only interim run I'd ever heard of in Philadelphia, now I had a one-performance play. At least I wasn't part of that legendary play so bad it closed between the first and second acts. Nor was I the designer of the mythic GLADIOLA GIRL, the theatre world's Flying Dutchman, a musical revue that went out on tour and never came back.

The timing of scenic elements that move in sight must be carefully arranged. The moment when we see or sense the picture to come, just before the scattered elements actually click together, must be a dawning pleasure, and only perfect sequences produce perfection.

You may have a clever design, but what is said in that design is what counts. A designer supports what is said or sung; you can't replace those elements with clever design. Perhaps in a horror movie our effects can be paramount.

Old theatre jokes can rise again. As I was walking down Forty-Fifth Street with Sam, an elderly woman stopped us. "Aren't you Sam Wanamaker?"

"Yes."

"You were wonderful!" (I guess in *The Blackboard Jungle*.) "But what have you done recently?"

EXERCISE

Can you tell a joke well? It's not so easy. Observe an expert: Watch the timing, the pauses, the sudden punch line. Sometimes the middle of the joke is the funniest part — you hear the verbal parenthesis. In the setting described in this chapter, or in a musical where the sets change in sight, the timing, the coming together of elements, is vital. Observe; practice.

CHAPTER TWENTY-TWO

Repertory, Classics, a Falling Out

I JOINED THE VIVIAN BEAUMONT at Lincoln Center when it was finally built and then came under the direction of Julius Irving. It was no longer a repertory theater, as Elia Kazan and Robert Whitehead had envisioned, just a theater devoted to classics. Even Jo, who designed the stage, had failed to put lively settings onstage. But director John Hirsch came down from Canada and insisted on pulling the acting area away from the proscenium and out onto the thrust stage, making the audience more of a surround to the action. His YERMA (I did the settings) established this and, as with the four-minute mile, once a barrier is broken it becomes possible to break it again and again.

Julius Irving was a fine man and a good producer — at least, he treated his help well — but he did not control budgets efficiently. I was responsible for getting sets onstage for the whole season, and Julius tended to give the first director anything she wanted, leaving my budgets depleted for the next three or four productions. I was often a villain — but anyone savvy understood, including Julius. This was another family for me, with the usual family scraps and squabbles, but a good family.

I designed the third and fourth seasons at the new Shakespeare Theater in Stratford, Connecticut. This was an unhappy theater. When I drove up from New York, I found myself slowing down for the last five miles, entering the parking lot in first gear. John Houseman ran the theater and was a good leader, but somehow cold, and perhaps that seeped down. I designed a HAMLET, among other things, and remember feeling that I was too young to design that play. The setting was good, but Brooks Atkinson didn't agree, and I respected his eye. He thought it too linear, too thin.

The clothes, designed by Alvin Colt, were like compact balls of wool, and beautiful, but they rested uneasily on my attenuated levels. They should have had a flow to them, some airiness to glide on these levels — or I should have beefed up the levels.

Jean Rosenthal was the lighting designer and technical director. I designed a fantastic curtain for the scene in the Queen's chamber when Polonius is stabbed. It was of intertwined images from the Book of Kells, and this was one of my favorite drawings. John Houseman saw this sketch first. "Wow!" he yelled, then, "*Wow.*" I was as pleased as I could be: John was not often demonstrative. But when Jean saw the sketch, her face clouded. It would be hard to mount and get onstage smoothly — but it could be done. Jean had breakfast every morning with John, and the next day the piece was out of the show. I was mad as hell, and later, in an interview, I let on that I had my disappointments. I didn't mention Jean by name but the interviewer guessed or snooped, and there it was, and that required a three-hour lunch with Jean (her call) to make up. I gave that sketch to Jack Landau, the director, who was soon murdered in Boston. I gave another sketch to Marc Blitzstein, who composed our music that year, and he was soon killed in a bar during a Caribbean vacation. I gave another to my father's marvelous secretary, who died soon after in an auto accident. I stopped giving away sketches from those years.

Jean was petite and handsome in that fine Susan Sarandon way, and always soft spoken. Her lighting for the New York City Ballet, for many years, was rightly applauded. One advantage she had in the old City Center is that you could not see the high stage floor from the best seats in the auditorium. The light fell on the dancers but the workaday stains where the light hit the stage floor beyond them was not seen. This makes the glow on the dancers magical. Jean also did Martha Graham's lighting and Martha considered her essential to the ballet's success. But Jean would have her way. It was shortly after my disappointment at Stratford that she was fired from her job at the New York City Ballet. Quintero, an encyclopedia of funny (if occasionally nasty) information, said this: "Jean comes into a quiet harbor like a big black submarine, and unseen she cuts all the mooring lines of the peacefully floating boats, then she reappears in a small birch-bark canoe, and as the boats crash into each other and sink, she says, 'Darlings, what's wrong? Sweethearts, what's happening?'"

Jean was fired because she disliked Ron Bates, a new stage manager at the ballet. Her initial comment, "He's too level-eyed for me," escalated into "It's him or me," and this was unacceptable to Lincoln Kirstein and George Balanchine.

WHAT I LEARNED

I was working at theaters that had permanent crews: New York City Center, Stratford, the Vivian Beaumont. Good crews must be respected. Suspicion and petty control don't work. Once, a manager said he was paying too much for burned-out lamps (bulbs) and wanted to see the corpses before paying for them. What could be easier than to go to other shows and collect a box full of burnouts to show the foolish man? Not to steal money, just to have a laugh. Another manager was presented with a bill for Pete Drambour's hat. Pete was chief carpenter at City Center. We all thought the hat was part of his head, but it fell off and was crushed under the wheels of a scenery truck. Pete billed the production for his ruined hat, but the manager giggled, "I don't pay for your clothes." When the next week's bills were presented, the manager was able to say, "No hat this week." "Oh, it's in there," said Pete. "You just can't see it."

I was advised by Jean Rosenthal, when we were friends, "Keep your fee high. That's the only way they'll listen to you." But I didn't push it high, and I felt I was heard.

I was learning common sense. This is such a difficult lesson in all endeavors, particularly when your passion and artistic ego are involved.

EXERCISE

This is something my favorite rabbi suggested: Spend a day carefully hearing every word said by you or others that demeans another person, even slightly, even in tone of voice, if not words. You'll be surprised at the number of times this happens. This exercise will improve your alertness. When you hear such a remark, count to ten, and then say the right thing. That could mean saying nothing — which is the ultimate command of language.

The rabbi failed — and as you read this book, you see that I fail also — but try anyway.

CHAPTER TWENTY-THREE

Too Much Control

A T CIRCLE IN THE SQUARE I designed an UNDER MILK WOOD for the talented director Bill Ball. He was so insistent on his desires — to the inch — that I was deprived of all artistic oxygen, and when the job was basically done, I asked to be excused. Bill had technical knowledge and could continue without me, which he had virtually done up to that point.

Bill wanted to show his genius independently of the show's success. There are ways to do this. As a small example, have your actors do some special action, such as a kiss, at a certain "ping" in the music. This is clearly director-arranged. The way a play starts, how doors open, and so on, are good moments that the actors, it seems, did not dream up. (Lighting and set designers, if unleashed, can also show their stuff independently at such moments.)

Soon after UNDER MILK WOOD, the downtown version of what would be the Vivian Beaumont was established. The desire was to have a repertory theater where, as with a ballet or opera company, three or more plays would be developed each season and they would alternate. Also, there would be a permanent company of actors studying and working together. Would it work? Boris Aronson once said that you cannot have a successful repertory theater in a city unless the theatre-goers have lived there for two generations.

The uptown construction would take time, and the desire to start a company was strong. So, a tin building, a large Quonset hut, was built on West Fourth Street, and Robert Whitehead and Elia Kazan began their work. José was hired to direct O'Neill's MARCO MILLIONS, and I

came along with him. Jo Mielziner designed the stage, and at one point we
shared it. Again I basked in the generosity of this man: we jointly designed
a turntable stage that could fit both his production and mine. MARCO
MILLIONS starred Hal Holbrook, before he became Mark Twain, and it
was well done.

For MARCO MILLIONS, I had the fun of designing a summer house
for the Grand Kahn that transformed in sight to a sailing junk. The bamboo ceiling beams pivoted to become masts, soaring upward; the summer
house ceilings, made of net, were then hauled up to become sails. This kind
of transformation is routine on a conventional stage, but this was out in the
open, without support from above. It surprised even me.

The costume designer was a spoiled, fashionable Venetian who spoke
no English when questioned about money. He didn't know how to row
a gondola. Luckily I did, and I taught one of our oarsman. This designer
picked out an astonishingly expensive fabric for the robes of the Grand
Kahn, played by David Wayne. (Leonora had a small part as a harem girl,
and her chief job was to remove David's wristwatch just before he went on.)
I found a cheap copy of the expensive fabric and had a pillow made for the
Kahn. It matched his costume, and when he rose from sitting it looked as if
his ass dropped off. It was a private joke, but even Bob Whitehead laughed.

After MARCO MILLIONS, José was not asked back to the Vivian Beaumont, but I was, and the next year I designed Molière's TARTUFFE in a
brilliant new translation by Richard Wilbur. Bill Ball was the director. He
asked for me, and I fell to the allure of flattery, despite our past troubles.
What really persuaded me was that Robert Whitehead was the producer,
and I would plunge into any project with that prince of a man.

It was again impossible to work for Bill. He wanted me to work in his
apartment/studio. He set up a drawing board, and we would meet there.
He was always late, arriving caped and surrounded by acolytes. He would
stand by the board. "Let's work on that entrance door, David. Sure. Now
let's see — if it's here, you'll want it three feet in from that edge — no,
make it two-foot nine; here, let me measure that — yes, but the door trim
should be six inches, plus a half-inch for the stop molding... hmm, so
that's three-feet three-and-a-half inches..." and on and on. Torture for

me. But the trouble was that after the door was built exactly as Bill wanted it, it was on the wrong side of the stage. When he realized that, it was already constructed, and Whitehead refused to spend the money to shift it to the other side. An ugly scene took place in the uptown rehearsal room, and when I escaped, I ran into Quintero on Seventh Avenue. Again, José seemed to get wind of events before they happened. "I hear you left Bill crying behind the piano."

"I dunno; I left."

"I didn't know it was a musical!"

When I could no longer bear Bill's micromanaging, I phoned him and said that meeting with him was like root canal work, and from then on I'd only see him every other day. Later that morning, I was summoned to Bob Whitehead's office. Bill was there, staging a frightful headache and going in and out of Bob's executive toilet to dampen the towel wrapped around his head. I told Bob, meanly, that Bill was fingerfucking the production to death, and Bill shot into the toilet. I asked to be excused from the lighting. My superb assistant, John Gleason, would take over. This was agreeable to all. I took the elevator down, and in the lobby I met Jane Greenwood, our costume designer. "Why you here?" I asked.

"I phoned Bill an hour ago and said I was cutting down my meetings with him; I was tired of looking at his costume postcards and he was fingerfucking the production to death."

Next, Kazan took on the directing of THE CHANGELING. The 1620s were not his cup of tea. But we had fun again, with Elia lying on my floor, talking about castles: dark places, rooms connected by narrow passages. We invented a set for our thrust stage, using narrow walkways connecting larger areas. It looked like one of those models of a chemical structure — lumps connected by rods. The set wasn't great, and nothing notable took place on it. I do remember clearly my Jesus, which floated above the set like an airplane suspended in a museum. He had a fifty-foot wingspan. At that theater, still downtown, we announced various procedures to the audience, the way "turn off your cell phones" is announced today. At the final dress rehearsal, a troubled Kazan said to me, "David, can we have Jesus's lips move during the no-smoking announcement?" His sense of humor was his lifeboat. I tended to fall asleep during long rehearsals, and one day he came and sat behind me. "Too bad you slept through that last scene, David. I've improved it a lot." We opened; the show was poor; and Elia and Bob were fired by some board of directors. After one bad show, and all the hope for the future. Amazing.

WHAT I LEARNED

Do not crowd your artists to the extinction of their desire to work. When you do this, as the modern saying goes, you suck all the oxygen out of the room. Years after the story in this chapter, Peter Good designed posters for the National Theatre of the Deaf. I criticized (helpfully, I thought) one of his rough sketches. "You're leaning on me too much. I want out," said Peter. I begged him to stay with us, and apologized. I did break the golden rule of apologizing, and offered an explanation: my clumsy interference with his process had come unconsciously from my own design life, where so many put in their oar. Peter understood, and his superb work for us continued.

I learned how tricky it can be to work with boards. Who fired Kazan and Whitehead? The board. In the nonprofit theatre world — not on Broadway, but in ballet and opera companies, and certainly this theater at Lincoln Center — a board of directors is necessary legally, and often financially: it raises money for company activities. The board has the power to hire and fire the artistic leaders and, by extension, many of the employees. Some artistic directors have had disagreements with their boards that were so serious that they quit. Edward Villella did a magnificent job establishing a brilliant ballet company in Miami, and I believed he had such a patent; it was *his* company. I was wrong. (I heard that one of the directors offered to underwrite a production if she could play the piano onstage.) Life became intolerable for Eddie, and he quit.

My company, the National Theatre of the Deaf, was established as a part of the O'Neill Center, and their board reigned but never interfered — or helped. After sixteen years, it became apparent that to survive we would have to become independent financially and establish our own board. My first step in this direction was to create an "artistic advisory board," which included Lillian Gish, Judy Collins, Itzhak Perlman, Arvin Brown, and Lucille Lortel among the members. This board had no legal status, but was a clear signal to the O'Neill Center that we could make it alone. If nothing else, this advisory board would be a buffer between the artistic director and the legal board, and signal that artistic decisions were not their job. In my case, I had a personal patent on the creation of the company, and a good bond with the government agency that funded us, and I never feared dismissal. In fact, I demanded that two bad chairpeople resign, and they did just that. (Usually I don't suggest this.)

Learn how to row a gondola — or anything else you will ask your actors to do. Be ready to demonstrate (or at least make a good imitation). I designed BILLY BUDD for the Brattle when I was still an undergraduate. At the base of the rigging, where we have what we call the chain plates, I designed a narrow platform. Sailors could swing onto it when starting to climb aloft, and Billy could make his final speech from there. I went to the great man-of-war, the USS *Constitution*, which is preserved in Boston, and tried this out. How exactly do you swing your body up there? I learned, and demonstrated to the director. He didn't use the idea, and I was disappointed but not suicidal.

There are four ways to swing open a conventional door. (That brings trouble that you can overcome if your stage is raked — sloped — because the door bottom hits that floor as it swings uphill.) When I helped on THE SLEEPING PRINCE in London, Olivier wanted a door to hinge downstage and open inward onto the stage. Thus, when the door opened, the actor opening it would be unseen behind it (masked, we say). Olivier, who would star in the play, wanted his gloved hand seen around the edge of the door before he himself appeared. A good detail.

EXERCISE

Time for another simple drawing exercise, one suggested by Frank Bevan at Yale. Take a dozen sheets of ordinary blank paper, and with any kind of marker (a pencil comes to mind), make some kind of mark on the sheet.

A dot, a small shape, or a squiggle. Any place. Now stare at the sheet, wait for the next mark to become clear, and make it. Do not make this mark until the place on the paper and the kind of mark become compelling! Study and stare again, until a third mark becomes necessary. This is the end of sheet number one; repeat eleven times. This is good for your sense of visual composition.

CHAPTER TWENTY-FOUR

Musical Disaster and Success

I DESIGNED TWO MUSICALS early on. (The label "musical comedy" can be a painful misnomer.) The main trouble for me was that these two shows were in preview at the same time — but in different cities. When I was in Detroit, I should have been in Philadelphia, and the other way around. I had an assistant in both places, and that might normally suffice — unless both projects are unraveling with anger.

A FAMILY AFFAIR was about a wedding. "Make a wedding" was my marching order. The set was a lacy structure, a fanciful mimicry of the decoration of a wedding cake. It went around on inner and outer turntables, supplying locales with small additional pieces that flew in or rolled on. It was pretty. We set up in the giant, cold Erlanger Theatre in Philadelphia, and trouble began with a terrible decision: the director wanted full orchestra rehearsals from the beginning. We were plunged into great — and unnecessary — expense. A good pit can rehearse quickly and doesn't need long days to grasp a score. To make matters worse, orchestra members take their breaks, or they did there and then, at a different time than the cast. Any given hour might not have one ten-minute rest, but two consecutive breaks, leaving only forty minutes of work time. Also, to re-rehearse a number, you usually need only nod at the rehearsal pianist, and his fingers hit the keys running. With a full pit, there is baton knocking to get everyone's attention, then page turning and baton lifting. By opening night, everyone was frustrated or furious — or both — and, worse, we were out of money.

Hal Prince came down and watched the show for a few nights, then the director was fired and Hal was hired. Hal had produced shows, but his great talent as a director was then unknown. This was his first time directing. I stayed in Philadelphia for those few days, and he wanted to talk to me, but he was absorbed reorganizing the cast and the book (that is, the script), and we never had our conference. I returned to Detroit and the other show. Soon Hal telephoned — at midnight. "David," he said, "I've put in changes. Friends have come down from New York to see them, and they all say that this could be a hit, but with your set, it can't be."

That was stunning information. If the set was that critical to the mess, he might have taken time to meet with me. But I couldn't blame him for such bad news. He was under great pressure, and I guessed these scapegoat ideas came from others. He had not seen the set as a key component to the disaster when I was with him. I was the "wictum."

I raced back to Philadelphia. "But Hal," I said, "there's no money left — not a penny for the big changes you want." He made suggestions, and we did what we could, reducing the set and painting it some dull color. "The trouble with this show is that it's about a wedding," I was told. Quite a difference from the initial charge.

So we limped into New York. The opening preview was dismal. My set looked like something that had been defecated by a giant bird. The writers were furious and asked for a meeting with Hal and me. The reviews had not come out, and when they did, the blame for a poor show would fall on them, not me. But that wouldn't be for another few days. Now, onstage just after the disappointed audience had filed out, I explained my wretched position. When I finished, Hal quickly said, "David is exactly right." I liked this marvelous man before that moment, and I've loved him ever since. We fixed what we could; we flopped; and I was not blamed.

Not that I've always been right. And being right doesn't help. I've not produced a *terrible* set since then, but I'm not proud of some mediocre work. But can a great set save a bad show? I remember a magnificent setting that surely extended the life of a show that was good anyway. That was Jo Mielziner's work for THE INNOCENTS, William Archibald's adaptation of Henry James's ghost story *The Turn of the Screw.* Yes, a ghost story — and a competent designer should be able to supply the important atmosphere for such a story. And Jo's haunted room, more than the plot, kept me on the edge of my seat. It was simple, with little furniture, the great staircase of an English country house curving up into mystery and darkness, and huge French doors looking outdoors, anticipating something awful gathering there. Jo's magical lighting caught the ghosts on the stairway and outside the doors in a way so subtle but so sure that we all saw them; yes, it was positive, but like a visual soft breath: the forms were there, but could not be described. (In his book *Designing for the Theatre,* Jo writes that he started creating that set from its lighting, not its architecture.)

I designed three more musicals after these first two, and lit a fourth, but my awful beginning with A FAMILY AFFAIR would have disqualified me if the other musical, NO STRINGS, had not succeeded for all of us. But even more, it changed the way musicals are presented. Success at the end after serious misery earlier.

Joe Layton asked for me for NO STRINGS. It was our first show together, and I did much work for Joe after this — those four musicals, and one play. Fred Voelpel did the clothes (this was before A MURDERER AMONG US), and there a lifetime friendship and partnership began. Fred dressed the dancers in decorative tights — not a new invention, but I believe it sparked the development of that style, which is still with us.

Joe was tall, dark, passionate, and clear-minded; there was no nonsense with his dancers or me. He wanted a show without any stops for scene changes. He had nineteen dancers and they could shift the small set pieces. The stagehand's union later objected to this, — actors or dancers couldn't take all their jobs away — and the basic contract was rightly adjusted. The stage was to be a large photo studio, with onstage rolling floodlights and paper backdrops that could be pulled down like window shades. Props and the onstage floodlights were moved about by the dancers in full sight. Upstage, large scoops (floodlights) were set behind a scrim, facing the audience, and could be turned on singly or in groups to make an abstract backdrop, varied and colorful.

Trouble began immediately for me. There were two large studios in New York then: Willy Nolan's shop in Brooklyn and David Steinberg's studio in Fort Lee, New Jersey. (Does that town ring a bell? Some of the earliest film work was done there until local stupidity drove it to California.) I submitted the plans of the musical to both shops. The foreman at Steinberg's, Peter Feller, who became my best friend for the remaining forty years of his life, ran that shop. He submitted through his boss a bid of $30,000. His problem was that the shop was too busy to take on the show, and much of this bid was overtime. Willy's shop was empty. I called him up: "Willy, if you're empty, what's all that hammering?"

"Oh, just fixing the floor, Dave."

Willy's bid was $19,000. A major musical for $19,000? Astonishing, and so far below budget. What a feather in my cap — in all of our caps — if Joe's concept and what I would add really did work. But Steinberg had always done Richard Rodger's shows, and he got the job. Pete was in distress, but despite his efforts, the set was shipped to Detroit unfinished: painting that was rushed, bits of fabric undone or unattached, casters that rolled poorly. Soon after, Pete quit Steinberg and started his own studio.

The show opened. A shambles. There was an oaf of a man who was everywhere, usually shouting, representing management. He had come over from George Abbott's operation and none of us dared name his area of skill. I was present when he yelled at Fred because the tights the girls were wearing had started to tear. "If" — said Fred, not known for tact — "if you would keep your fat ringed fingers out of their crotches, that would not be happening." The dancers who heard this applauded. Then I lost my best electrician. One of the dancers had been doing "extra work" with someone high in management, and then she was caught in bed with this electrician as well. She and the person in management were both married. The electrician was not. But who was fired? Figure it out.

There was more. I wasn't getting light out of the ancient instruments owned by management. (Usually instruments, dimmer boards, and cables were rented, but some established producing firms owned their supply, and rented it to themselves at high rates, paid for by the investors.) I ill-advisedly turned on a few circuits on a quiet afternoon to examine a dozen of these old warriors. I was spotted and yelled at in a restaurant that night by the chap mentioned before, a purple-necked, public dressing-down. He claimed that I was sneakily trying to discredit the electrical staff. Worse, I had muttered that so much trouble was caused by that $11,000 gap. Hmm, where had the money gone? Are kickbacks truly a victimless crime even if you stay so far within the budget? No — my hastily built stuff didn't work and I was blamed. Not to mention the gypped investors.

I learned later that Rodgers wanted to fire me and phoned Oliver Smith, who turned down the job, and reportedly said that Joe Layton and I would pull it off, "just let them work."

Work we did. When not in Philadelphia, I spent all day — and some nights — onstage, painting and fixing. I became so tired that I fell asleep while sitting on top of a ladder. Just a six-foot stepladder. Richard Kiley caught me.

Despite all these troubles, we knew it was a good show. Rodgers had written excellent lyrics as well as the music. One person who disliked him admitted it was good: "That man sure holds a thermometer up the asshole of America." In somewhat the same vein but with real admiration, Peter Matz, musical boss and arranger, called me over one day to the rehearsal piano. "David, listen to this transition I've made between two songs." He played a complex bridge from minor to major — fast, tricky, and brilliant. "Well, dammit, I took it to the boss and played it and he admired it. He said, 'Great, Peter, but what about this?'" Peter then hit one note on the piano. "Just one note! And it's better!"

Dick (as he preferred to be called) remained outwardly calm. This was not a bad show with a bad set, like A FAMILY AFFAIR, but a good show unattractively mounted. Joe and I did some redesigning, such as adding small trees that the dancers could move to make a Paris park or avenue, and we rethought the lighting. Dick approved. These new items were made and shipped to Detroit. Slowly the set improved. In fact, it became good — and by the time we moved to New Haven, it was fresh and exciting.

One interesting alteration was made toward the end of the Detroit run. The stage floor had become crowded with spike marks, a confusing morass of little numbers and letters indicating the act and scene where a tree or lamppost should be spotted (placed), with speed and in half-light. I repainted the floor with colorful graffiti. Instead of numbers and letters, airplanes, cars, trains, parachutes, dogs and cats and canaries, a sun and moon, and a hundred more pictures filled the forty-by-thirty-foot surface. Good clues, they instantly became easier and more secure for the dancers who carried and spotted the props.

We opened in New Haven to acclaim. Dick said to me, "We've opened too late in the season for you to get a Tony award, but something better's coming." That was the Critics' Circle award. Quiet but grand.

As I mentioned before, the show had great importance in changing the way musicals are presented, credit to Joe Layton. Before NO STRINGS, musicals or any show with multiple sets either changed them with an intermission, the custom of opera, or had a quick curtain-down interval, as in THE LATE GEORGE APLEY. In musicals (in all shows), we divide the stage into three areas: "one," far downstage, "two," from downstage to midstage, and "three," the whole stage. If you needed to change the big set, you ran a curtain across, separating "one" from upstage, and a "crossover scene" took attention downstage of this curtain while the big set was being changed. The curtains could be amusingly painted. Scenes were invented to play "in one," and even songs, such as "On the Street Where You Live" in MY FAIR LADY, took place there. I remember the comic scene of a lady followed by a man struggling to carry her giant packages in GUYS AND DOLLS. Finally, the curtain would open to reveal the new full-stage splendor. In MY FAIR LADY, the curtain in one opened to reveal a glorious ballroom on a turntable, its parts still moving to cleverly join together. That was Oliver Smith's beautiful work, what we called "a gasper." The point is that after NO STRINGS, this was deemed an antique practice. Now all scenic moves are made cleverly in full sight. NO STRINGS made that change.

WHAT I LEARNED

Keep your mouth shut; do your job. Or, if you can't keep it shut, at least don't complain with it. Again, do your job.

There is a lesson in that floor that I painted for the dancers. Take notice of ideas like this. Be attentive to the cast. Often a designer's work can be adjusted to help them. Think of helping the cast as one of your principal jobs.

I learned the following in conversation with Dick Rodgers about a difficult scene I was trying to design. "David, it's okay to be at an elegant formal dinner party and say 'shit!' — as long as you mean it!"

The cast and crew of NO STRINGS felt we were a community — a family — however contentious. The morning after we opened, I had an impacted molar removed, and that afternoon I played our weekly softball game. We had a "Broadway league," but there were off-Broadway teams as well, and producing organizations could also join. Before the NO STRINGS team was organized, I played for Circle in the Square. One spring I played for MY FAIR LADY. They needed a second baseman and allowed me to claim that I was Oliver Smith. G. C. Scott was a formidable pitcher, and I'm proud of the one hit I made off him — or did the shortstop just fall down on his way to the limp grounder? Henry Fonda — such a pleasant man — often came out to watch us play in Central Park. He hunched over on a bench, his thin legs twined. José could do that also.

This was fun but it didn't last, at least for me. Some of the business or stage managers who organized the teams were competitive, and ringers began to appear. It was rumored that when replacement dancers or understudies auditioned for a show, their athletic abilities were considered. Teams got better; girls stopped playing; fun tapered off. Players appeared who weren't theatre professionals, and when the rosters were challenged, there were false claims of these players doing a bit part or having understudied — or even having ushered. One afternoon, I played on a team with a fantastic player, far better than the rest of us. That was Willy Mays. My teammate. (This is important for my résumé.)

One cause of my musical comedy misery was overcommitment. I should not have taken on two big shows at once, at least, not so early in my career. After this, besides being more cautious, I realized I needed to be more generous in hiring assistants, and I should not be so possessive about doing the lighting myself.

EXERCISE

Painting the stage floor for NO STRINGS was a good idea, and so helpful to the cast. Now pretend you are blind and walk around your house or apartment. How many steps between here and there? What clues guided you? Now (no longer blind) pace out a distance. Can you accurately pace off yards? This is a useful skill.

CHAPTER TWENTY-FIVE

More Musicals and a Fantastic Preview

FTER THE success of NO STRINGS, I designed Richard Rodgers's next musical, with Joe Layton again directing. TWO BY TWO was based on Clifford Odets's play THE FLOWERING PEACH. Danny Kaye starred as Noah. Joe's idea was that God's voice, giving instructions to Noah, would be seen as dozens of huge projected images of religious paintings, flashing quickly on the sky. My idea was that Noah lived in an assembly of tumbledown shacks and crates, and the Ark would assemble magically from these. All of that worked, but there were not many instructions from God in Act II, and I might have done something more interesting and useful on the large sky. There's nothing wrong with a handsome sky, but if it's been used in an interesting way for a period of time, it becomes noticeably dull when it simply sits there.

The real trouble was with Danny Kaye, in my opinion. He came to believe that his own improvised wit was superior to what Dick and the joke inventors had done (there can be such writers, hired specifically to invent jokes). His ad-libbing threw other cast members into confusion. An image remains in my mind of Danny striding about in his plaster cast—he had broken his leg—while the petrified actor-singers waited to invent some flat response to his next surprise sally. If we'd had another Noah, perhaps less famous or fatuous, the show might have run and run.

Another musical, again with Joe Layton, was DRAT! THE CAT!, about a cat burglar, played by the gorgeous Lesley Ann Warren. I wandered during the design process, and whatever slow progress I made was nicknamed "Drab the Cat" by the producers. That was a wake-up. I stopped drawing shapes and found a bright color scheme, and then suddenly new shapes appeared. That's a good lesson.

DRAT! THE CAT! started in Philadelphia. It finally had colorful settings, and I was pleased. They were complex, and we were given a full week to assemble them and get them moving. Since NO STRINGS, all the curtains, drops, and units had to shift swiftly in full sight. The difficulty in Philadelphia was that the assembling crews were poorly assigned. The carpenters had too much to do and the electricians too little. This was the fault of our own crew chiefs, those bosses who travelled with us and directed the local men. For example, there was an elevator in the orchestra pit, and we had to excavate two feet of concrete to fit it in. Was that a mechanical unit for the carpenters, or an electrical unit? It was electrically controlled and could have gone either way.

This was so frustrating that on the fifth day, there was a mild fistfight. I couldn't resist joining (as the Irish say, "Is this a private fight, or can anyone join in?") and ended up carrying one electrician, still lightly and aimlessly flailing, off into the wings.

In our production, two balconies, one above the other, jutted out from each side. A bridge spanning the stage moved up and down to connect them. Varied curtains played in a rectangular opening midstage, an inner proscenium. One of these curtains swung upstage as an awning, roofing a garden setting. The orchestra rode around the stage on a two-tiered bandstand with frilly Victorian details.

A full set-up crew could be "knocked off" only after the scenery was together and working and the lights were focused. Then all the extra local men hired to set up, to hang scenery and lights and to focus them went home, and you trimmed down to the "running crew," who worked the show in performance. Yes, you could still make minor adjustments and repairs, but you didn't cheat the bigger local crews out of a few hours' work by doing a rushed and sloppy set-up or focus. Generally, once sets were assembled, you might need two or three more hours for focus, and then the set-up was over.

Finally in preview, facing our first New York audience, we were set to go.

Stagehands stood at each of the four balconies, ready to push on screens. The bandstand, up left, was ready to move across to center stage and then, with musicians madly playing, turn and head downstage to rendezvous with the conductor as he rose grandly on the elevator. All was ready, or getting ready. There were six cue lights plus the curtain light. These small red lights, positioned where stagehands had to initiate something, were turned on at about the two-minute warning, then went out to signify "Go!" But a fuse blew and the lights snapped out early. The curtain went up. Two stagehands pushed on their screens; two were not fooled. The bandstand lurched onstage, three musicians racing after it and jumping on as it pivoted downstage. The unfortunate conductor rose magnificently but his bright jacket was not yet on — in fact he had stepped into his suspenders and was bent over and squirming, tied in a knot.

The music stopped, which was good because the musicians had started at different times. There was silence except for laughter from Fred and me, standing in the back of the auditorium. We both tended to laugh when things went terribly wrong and there was nothing we could do about it. The brave stage manager stepped out. "Ladies and gentlemen, due to technical difficulties, the show has begun." He urged patience. The conductor sank out of sight, the bandstand retreated, the curtain came in, and in five minutes we tried again, with success. What's the lesson here? Face disaster; make it amusing if possible (but don't trivialize it). Climb out.

I also designed PLATINUM, starring Alexis Smith, and her first entrance was down a circular stair. These can be confusing to design. Mine was easy to descend, but the arms-up "Hello" to the audience was made as Miss Smith stepped off facing upstage. This would have been easy to correct by adding another step, but coming off that she would have smashed into a wall. The thing should have spiraled clockwise, not counterclockwise — and we changed to that, tediously.

About twenty years later, I went to a musical at Goodspeed, the opera house near my Connecticut home. The curtain rose on an exact copy of my PLATINUM set, now being used by another designer for another musical. Suddenly I realized that my own set had been a copy, or at least a close relative, of a scenery system I had used at Stratford, which had created many figurations with simple movements. Imitation is called flattery. How does that apply if you unconsciously copy yourself?

Joe Layton also asked me to design the musical BARNUM and I went to see the producer. We had a pleasant meeting, and at the end, the foolish man said, "Wait a moment Oliver Smith is coming up. We'll all talk, and then I'll decide who will be our designer." I had learned enough to say, "No hassle, Oliver will design it." Down in the lobby I met Oliver, told him the story, and he never went up in the elevator. Another designer got the job.

WHAT I LEARNED

From Danny Kaye's behavior, I learned how a selfish ego can destroy the hard work and hopes of many.

I learned how funny and delightful Madeline Kahn could be. Fred had designed her costumes in TWO BY TWO, and one pair of tight short pants was covered in sequins. She missed her entrance during our dress rehearsal, but soon appeared and walked downstage center to apologize. "I'm sorry," she said. "But a sequin had entered my system."

Designing DRAT! THE CAT! reinforced my notion that the mind doesn't always lead the pencil; the pencil can lead the mind. There are theories relating to this. Salvador Dalí wrote that he would sit in a comfortable chair holding a pencil or some small object, and when he dozed off, the object would fall from his fingers and land with a sharp sound on a plate he had placed on the floor. The mind, as it suddenly woke from its relaxed state, would produce an original idea. I never had luck with this, but if I pondered a problem as I went to sleep at night, the morning often brought a solution.

Things change. I was using the colors Roger Furse used, watercolors in small jars made by a company in London. Each year, I sent for the renewals I needed, but one year there was only a letter saying that Mr. Jenkins, who mixed those colors, had died, and they would no longer be offered. About this time, the mat board I used for my renderings was also discontinued. I've never been happy with my colored drawings since then.

EXERCISE

Do what Salvador Dalí suggests: Let yourself doze off and be startled awake. Does this work to produce an original idea in your mind? Ponder a specific problem just before you sleep at night. Is a solution in your mind when you wake up?

CHAPTER TWENTY-SIX

We Knew Famous People

I OWE QUINTERO (and Leonora) of course) my start in New York. We were a team for more than nineteen productions, half off-Broadway or opera, half Broadway plays. But do not be totally fooled by the equality that "team" implies. Yes, we designers are important at first, the eager right-hand men or women of a director as the staging of a production is conceived. We are bright enough, knowledgeable enough, and witty enough, and are invited to dinners, but we are not important enough to hire stars and other actors, or to rent theaters or billboards.

This book is not intended as a memoir, but the resemblance is unavoidable. My hope is that the stories I include will illustrate the life a designer may lead. We spent evenings with legendary people, but the conversations could concern such mundane topics as where to send one's children to school, and I often fell asleep. Once Balanchine asked Leonora and me to supper with Igor Stravinsky and Peter Brook (there, I've dropped names) but they spoke only Russian. The one English statement I remember was Leonora's request for the salt.

An interesting aspect of our profession is that a memorable job is not forgotten. One evening, at a benefit, I had a long and delightful conversation with a beautiful older woman. I found out later she was Fay Wray, the actress who squirmed in the great ape's tender hands in the original *King Kong*. Remember Julie Hayden, who was wonderful in THE GLASS MENAGERIE? She did little else, but she is remembered. And Vivian Blaine from GUYS AND DOLLS? My point is that an artist should be remembered for his or her finest work. Tennessee Williams wrote unsuccessful plays later in his life and some people grumbled. Shape up, ingrates! Do not scorn a man who gave us — in my opinion — our best play.

Most famous people have earned their fame. I designed a show for Hume Cronyn and we became friends. At a dinner he told this story: In the film *The Seventh Cross*, he had played a young factory worker who was harboring a spy (Spencer Tracy). One morning, as the young worker starts on his bicycle ride to work, an open car full of ss men pulls up, and one shouts "Get in!" Hume's character is terrified, of course — what can lie ahead but torture and death? He gets into the car. After the rehearsal, Hume asked the director, "Should I try to pull the bicycle into the car?"

I started to cry. My wife had just died, and dinners like this had been arranged so that I could be with friends. (Actually, I believe they wanted to know whether, without Leonora, I could complete a full sentence.) I couldn't stop blubbering, and fled the dinner, with Hume and our hostess patting me on the back at the door. This was the first time I had "lost it" since Leonora's death.

In this story from a man I revered as a director as well as an actor and friend, I found a touchstone of what it's all about: a young artist exploring his character and coming up with a powerful insight. He clutches the only thing he has left as he is dragged away. It is a scene of wrenching loss. The bicycle is the symbol; the effort to clutch it is the action. This seems a small event, but it suddenly bursts open the door to compassion. That's what we do! Actors, directors, designers, all of us.

Many theatre workers, myself included, can take a day off when in, say, Cleveland, to go to the park, to a museum. Others, and I knew many, were so devoted to their work that on days off, they would visit the empty theater, review the script and all their notes, and seek others to "go over lines." This was how Leonora approached theatre. She adored all aspects of the art. Hume's story created this emotional result.

Back to Hume. The director did not accept the suggestion, but I see a bridge shot of the car speeding away with the bicycle in the foreground, wheel spinning, lying in the road. Just a second or two, neither original nor profound, but a start. Do better.

I designed an early Tennessee Williams play, PORTRAIT OF A MA-DONNA, for Hume. It ends with the lady being escorted out of her apartment by two men who have come to take her to an asylum. Mr. Williams ends the play with a sympathetic speech by one of these men, and then they "go out slowly, closing the door, and the light fades out." That's good, but not great, I thought, bringing down the curtain on an empty stage. I suggested that one of the men brush against her rocking chair as he exited, and we see her empty chair rocking gently in the shabby, deserted room as the curtain comes in, slowly. Not a giant effect, but an appropriately scaled finale.

When fading to end a scene or coming up to begin one, the speed, timing, and intensity of lighting are important tools. Curtains also. Sometimes you may just have an instruction that says "down curtain." Then, if you have a choice, what kind of curtain? One that simply goes up and down? Closes in from the sides? Or sweeps in rather grandly (operatically) from the upper corners? Or perhaps no curtain, just a fade? How long a pause before you bring it up for the curtain calls? This is a good exercise for a designer or director: as you read a play, visualize how you would end or begin a scene, using all these tools.

Here is a strong use of light to end a play: In Terence Rattigan's SEP-ARATE TABLES, the elderly residents of a pension sit in frigid isolation under the harsh lights of their dining room. Events bring them to feel some sympathy for each other, and the angel of compassion enters the room. The harsh light dims. Tiny table lamps, unnoticed before in the brightness, now cast their warm pools. The room, the characters, the play are charmed as the curtain falls. Whose idea was it? The playwright's? The director's, one of the designers', an actor's? Good ideas can come from any member of the team.

W. Somerset Maugham, in his engrossing *The Summing Up*, offers this: "I have known a number of actors very well. I have found them good company. Their gift of mimicry, their knack of telling a story, their quick wit, make them often highly entertaining. They are generous, kindly, and courageous. But I have never quite been able to look upon them as human beings. I have never succeeded in achieving any intimacy with them. They are like crossword puzzles in which there are no words to fit the clues. The fact is, I suppose, that their personality is made up of the parts they play. . . . Make-believe is their realty."

I strongly disagree. The fine performers we knew were centered people.

I certainly would not wish to deny them burial in consecrated ground because they had no souls, the fate of many actors over several centuries. Or perhaps you've seen those boardinghouse signs, usually quaint reproductions, saying "No theatricals," supposedly a result of anger because Lincoln was shot by John Wilkes Booth, an actor. My guess is that today we study our characters in a deeper way than was customary in Maugham's day. Today you might say we study inner motivations more than mimicking outer behavior. If there is an afterlife, God could do no better than to have Colleen Dewhurst, Hume Cronyn, Jessica Tandy, and so many others as Her ushers — everyone would be thoughtfully shown to their perfect seat.

WHAT I LEARNED

I want to say that these famous people I've mentioned were in many ways ordinary human beings — yes, with talent, magnetism, charisma, call it what you will. Some of them were brilliant; some not so bright, but with the knack of transformation. Most of them — in fact, all of those I cared for — did not take their success for granted, but acknowledged the luck that is needed to rise in our competitive industry. And they were encouraging to others.

We all took pleasure in each other's company. Some in Hollywood filmland are famous for difficult work habits, but fewer on New York stages are cranky. One rising star was remarkably cold to me and the stage crew, and they rewarded her with a rare discourtesy: they went up to the fly floor and looked down at her as she made a quick "skin change" in a screened-off ceilingless area. I was once at the New London railroad station when a famous dancer and choreographer arrived to meet a substantial donor to the Connecticut College dance festival. She mistook me for him. When she realized her mistake, she spun away from me so abruptly that I was certain she had wrenched her back. When I tried to imitate this rudeness to my staff I did exactly that, and spent a day in bed.

Be attentive to workers even if they don't advance your career. You may climb up the ladder, but someday you'll have to climb back down. Have friends to greet you.

Learn to write well, I beg my grandchildren. Then you can reach out to the world with your discoveries. One such man was the mythologist Joseph Campbell. With his cheerful permission, the Theatre of the Deaf developed a play from his *The Hero with a Thousand Faces,* which Larry Arrick adapted and directed. Joe saw it when we performed at the Los Angeles Olympics in 1984. He came backstage and explained to us what we had done. He found fascinating symbols and connections beyond our awareness. I relate this because there is a moral: make a good play with taut and telling relationships between people and, as in our own private lives, meanings we never intended or fathomed will appear and nourish us.

EXERCISE

What is your relationship, or attitude, to people who you believe are less educated, less well read? Even less smart? Are you maybe just a bit superior? To stagehands, perhaps? To anyone who is doing things not exactly your way? Lose this, lose this, lose this. Fast.

CHAPTER TWENTY-SEVEN

Concrete at Last

A MURDERER AMONG US had only one performance. A few dozen other plays or musicals I designed lasted only the rest of the week after a Tuesday opening. Too often during those years I saw my set of the previous week being carted up Eighth Avenue en route to the dump in Jersey. Naturally, I aspired to design something that didn't leave town quickly. While Sam Wanamaker was involved in his giant project in London, re-creating the Globe Theatre, I was designing a small theater in Oklahoma City.

The Ford Foundation's arts leader, Mac Lowry, had predicted accurately in the late fifties that the sixties would bring on a spate of theater building. These new theaters would be poorly designed, he assumed. So why not give grants to eight teams, each consisting of a scenic designer and an architect? The results would be published as a booklet — *Eight Ideal Theaters* — and might be influential.

I was appointed as a set designer, and my partner was the architect and architecture critic Peter Blake. We decided to do a small "open stage" theater, of particular interest to me, a lover of the old Circle in the Square. We met and sketched. At the third meeting Peter leaped from his chair with a cry. "Aha! I've got it!" And so he had. He drew a rectangular stage, surrounded on all sides by seats on the floor and above on a balcony. The trick was that the floor position of the seating was lowered so that the eye of the first-row patron was at stage level. This could bring the balcony lower: it could be only five feet above the stage. We checked sight lines. It would work. Our charge was to supply simple drawings and a model to the Ford Foundation. The model was beautifully made by a company specializing in that work. The other seven models were gorgeous, too, and after the exhibition and publication of the booklet, I collected them and gave them to the O'Neill Center, where they were exhibited — and subsequently lost. (That's the only curator I know who lost an entire exhibition.)

When Peter Blake and I finished our design, we had money left over from the grant. I phoned Mac Lowry's assistant, Marcia Thompson, and asked how to give it back. "We have no pathway for that," she said. "Have a party for all concerned." And we did that.

Years later, after Mac Lowry died and Marcia took his place, the Theatre of the Deaf was embezzled. I applied to various foundations for a "bridge grant" to help us through a specific period. The Ford grant came through late on the same day that another grant was announced and accepted. I told Marcia I could not accept hers because the wording of the application for the grant was so specific. She was surprised, but I remembered an old story. A southern planter approached the boy wooing his daughter. "Young man, are your intentions honorable or dishonorable?" "You mean," said the astonished swain, "I have a *choice?*" I was rewarded with another grant from her, a year later.

Mack Scism had established a storefront theater in his Oklahoma City, and the Ford Foundation deemed it good to give him a handsome theater building. This was a small city at that time: about six hundred thousand residents. The theater would have six hundred seats. Would a fine building inspire attendance, enough to give it a continued life, and would it boost the cultural life of the city? Mack was content with individual shows, not a revolving repertory using the same actors (that's what the Brattle was, almost, and that's what Kazan and Whitehead failed to establish). Mack wanted to use stars, but the stars that could attract an audience in Oklahoma City were not from stage or film, but from television: soap-opera stars and so forth.

I was hired as the theater designer. Mack and I searched for the architect partner. He preferred John Johansen to Peter Blake, and we began. I worked on the design first, and the idea was good. The stage was a thrust, with seats surrounding it on three sides. The seating would be in balcony trays or boxes that hovered about a foot over the stage. The stage could be built in many different shapes, and could be rolled off under the seats. A partial stage or a whole new stage could then be rolled in. You could also tuck the stage under the seating trays and arrange floor seats facing a proscenium. Also, actors could enter from under the trays, climbing onto the stage from any direction. This was an improvement over most thrust stages, where the entrance ramps were fixed.

The essence of one school of architecture is to put in place the needed function — in this case, the theater space for the audience and actors — and then wrap it tightly with outer walls. The function of the building is intended to show through the walls. This opposes the tradition of building a rectangular building and then fitting whatever is needed inside it. The rub is that architects want their buildings to look their best from the outside. John wrapped my stage, and yes, the outside reflected the interior. But then he decided he wanted changes to the exterior, and he made them, so now the interior reflected the exterior. But we had good fun and glorious arguments, and produced a stage and a wrap-around that pleased both of us, and Mack.

Ten years after we designed it, the theater was built. It was delayed because it was part of a city plan, and a city plan is all too often a scheme whereby those in power who own real estate juggle it until they realize maximum profit. In the sixties, there was no shortage of powerful people in Oklahoma City. Some of the older "bull elephants," as Mack named them, had been little children sitting in the backs of the wagons during the famous land rush of 1889.

The theater finally opened in 1970, and it was fine. Mac Lowry had helped in the final phases of the construction fund-raising. He had somehow unearthed a letter from a young engineer, addressed to a businessman in Oklahoma City. It said, in essence, that the young man appreciated the better job and higher salary offered in Oklahoma City, but his wife insisted that he take the job offered in Tulsa, because the culture of that city promised a better upbringing for their children. Did Mac Lowry forge that letter? Anyway, money poured in, and the building was completed. Would it eventually give the city the culture it lacked?

About a year later Mack Scism's board betrayed him, and he quit. I offered him a job with the Theatre of the Deaf, and he said that I'd worked loyally for him for ten years, so he'd come and work for me. We were enthusiastic partners for over ten years until he died.

As for the theater in Oklahoma, after Mack Scism it became the home of fundamentally amateur managers, and they filled in the spaces at the edge of the stage, freezing it and all its advantages. They said it was dangerous, all those edges. The downstage edge of any stage is a perilous cliff, with the bright lights dazzling you. It's perhaps a three-foot drop, perhaps six or seven into the orchestra pit. But not tumbling off is part of an actor's job. As for the work I did, I wouldn't mind now if the whole theater could be carted up Eighth Avenue to the dump. The saying is that God punishes us by granting our wishes: there is my wish, its spoiled version preserved forever in concrete. Well, maybe not forever — there's a move to tear the whole thing down, and there is a Japanese saying, "Always is almost never forever."

I continued to design or consult on theaters, and my advice was usually ignored. As an example, the plans of an academic theater in upstate New York were shown to me. I questioned the two dressing rooms, each capable of containing sixteen actors. I said that I knew of no play where there were sixteen men and sixteen women in the same cast. Make one room twenty, I said, and the other eight. This will leave space for a small third room to be used by an occasional guest star. The architects replied that you couldn't use the same room for men in one show and women in the next, because the women wouldn't use or want to see the urinals in the men's toilet. "But you don't need urinals," I said. "I've raised a girl and a boy, and there's no urinal in my house."

"The building code demands urinals in the men's room," they said.

"That's for audience use," I offered. "It doesn't apply to dressing rooms. And you could put the toilets between and connected to both dressing rooms and lock or indicate different doors as desired." All true, but I lost.

However, I did campaign for more ladies' stalls in the audience restrooms, because I'm distressed to attend the theatre at Lincoln Center or on Broadway and see dignified women with festive togs and full bladders standing in long lines in the lobby, while the men quickly go in and out.

One place where I've prevailed in this matter is in our town's new synagogue. There's even a plaque inside the ladies' room, starting "Gentle user," and crediting Leonora for her concern with what women deserve, meaning more stalls.

I was helpful to a theater in Sydney, Australia. It was well designed, but was only a stage and an auditorium. Add a rehearsal room and it could be the home of an Australian national theatre, I said. That alone earned my fee. I remember three things about that work:

First, when I went down there, I spent time in the architect's office, on the other side of the great harbor bridge from the theater site. There is an amusement park by the architect's office, and the window in the conference room looked out to the very top of the main dip of the roller coaster. That is where the riders look down the steep slope to their oncoming deaths. You saw only the heads of the riders out the window, and every ten minutes you would witness thirty terrified, disembodied and screaming heads flashing by only ten feet away.

Second, the old theater, I believe it was called the Victoria, was to be torn down to make space for a new skyscraper. The unions, strong and tight, refused to build the new structure unless the old theater's union jobs were replaced. The developer solved this by building a theater in the new building. That's when I was hired as a consultant. When asked what my fee would be, I said that the builder should sponsor a tour of my company, the Theatre of the Deaf. Leonora was upset because we needed the money ourselves, but I was too consumed with promoting the company to listen.

Third, my company eventually played in the great harbor theater, the one that has the beautiful wings or nuns' headdresses overlapping. There the outside did indeed shape the inside, and the theater spaces nestled inside are unfortunately not the best.

Balanchine asked me to consult on the building of the New York State Theater (now the David H. Koch Theater). The theater was to be shared by the New York City Ballet and the New York City Opera — and the opera's demands were different than the ballet's. The opera wanted platforms built in to the stage that would rise as needed. These were costly and contradictory to the kind of floor dancers need. They also wanted bridges (walkways between pipes up in the flys), which Balanchine and I felt would take up too much space. These things could all be added later, we argued, let's just start simply. The opera also wanted towers downstage on each side of the proscenium, with ladders in them. Spotlights could be operated from different levels. These were three feet wide, and would take up valuable space just upstage of the proscenium. Tom DeGaetani, who had been the technical director at Tanglewood, argued on our side. Tom liked big words. "This theater isn't as big as the German opera houses," he stated. "There, when you don't want the towers, you can just articulate them upstage." Ronnie Bates, our stage manager, who was from Oklahoma and lacked fancy words, said, "Yeah, but what if you just wanna get rid of the muthafuckas?" We won all that, but two problems remained.

First, Betty Cage, the ballet's capable and delightful general manager, who brought Tarot cards when negotiating with the stuffy, wouldn't move to the proposed new building unless the architect, Philip Johnson, pierced his marble wall and gave her a window. She prevailed. I was not involved, but the lesson stuck, and I've argued for windows ever since. A particular favorite demand is to have windows in the costume room, where sewing elves toil day and night. They should see the seasons change. I succeeded at this in a Florida theater — where the seasons don't change much anyway.

Second, beside the ballet and opera, Richard Rodgers was to have a musical theatre, a third of the pie in the New York State Theater. His demand was for more seating: he wanted two more rows. In the broad auditorium, this would yield over seventy additional orchestra seats, and that's a lot of income. To make room for this on the auditorium floor, the orchestra pit would have to be pushed six feet further under the stage. That's not hard, but its upward opening into the auditorium would be narrowed by that six feet. German sound engineers appeared. They showed us large charts with vibration lines circling out from the musicians' places and stated that the pit, even if half under the stage, would produce its sounds as perfectly as before. Balanchine was smart at things of this sort. He let the silence after the presentation go on for an extra beat. Then he said, "But will my dancers onstage hear the music as well?" Quiet in the room. No answer, no charts anticipating that question, no extra rows of seats — and no Richard Rodgers.

A few years after this, I had the honor to consult on a theater being designed by Marcel Breuer. He had fascinating ideas, but I believed he couldn't meet the budget. "You know, David," he said, "that's always the case, but we architects usually ignore budgets and design buildings so appetizing that they cannot be resisted. Then the extra money is raised."

"Yes," I said, "that may be the modus of architects, but you are designing for a Catholic college for women, run by nuns." It was my experience (for by now I was selling touring appearances by my company) that nuns were good at saying no, and surely that was one reason many of them succeeded at being nuns. "We'll see," he said. Unfortunately for a major work by that good artist, and for my small portion, I was right.

WHAT I LEARNED

I learned that intimacy depends on the closeness of the first row to the stage and actors. The audience is something of a unit, and if the first row is close, it all feels close. The fourth row, for example, will feel close if the first is close, but it will feel distant if the first is not snug to the stage.

Was it silly for the Rodgers organization to refuse participation in Lincoln Center because of two rows of seats? I understand how negotiators can turn cranky over the smallest points, and surely there were other considerations. But to give up a goldmine because it isn't quite huge enough? What a wonderful venue it could have been for revivals of those brilliant shows.

During the negotiations, and because I was producing (doing business) more than designing, I was struck by the simple truths of the old imperishable and instructive fables. How often I saw, enacted in the most obvious way, "The Dog and the Bone"; "The Goose That Laid Golden Eggs"; "The Fox and the Grapes." And, sadly, how often I forgot them myself. Please pay attention to these stories.

When designing a theater, beware of the duct workers. These cheerful tin cowboys will run a duct from upstage to downstage and eliminate any possibilities of flying your scenery. Or how about connecting the scenery construction shop to the stage via duct? Then the minimal fart gently released in the workroom will become a trumpet call at the matinee. In one theater, Jo Mielziner designed a door forty feet high to let tall scenery pass from the shop onto the stage. Quick as a wink (at midnight, he guessed) an air duct shot across it, cutting it in half. Then scenery only twenty feet high could pass through. Easily fixed — even funny.

EXERCISE

Reread the great fables. Yes, "The Dog and the Bone," "The Goose That Laid Golden Eggs," the lot of them. They're still with us for a reason.

CHAPTER TWENTY-EIGHT

Opera Tales

I STARTED DESIGNING OPERAS with José Quintero. We went to City Center with an opera concerning Saint Joan, and nothing about it was distinguished. Julius Irving was in charge, and after the dress rehearsal, he phoned me at home to ask a question about our budget. This was followed by a call from his business manager, who had a question about a light cue. Finally, his technical director called to ask about a costume that troubled him. (I had not done them, but he called me anyway.) It was a circus, but pleasant and respectful, and I liked all of these men.

Then the Metropolitan Opera established a second company. Call it a triple-A ball team: a source of talent for the main company, and a touring outreach. The magnificent soprano Risë Stevens was the boss. Again, I followed José to the Met. We opened this company's shows at John Johansen's theater at Butler University in Indianapolis, which out-of-town crews called "Indian No Place." We questioned how this city became a city, without a river or distinguishing landmark of any kind, and before the auto race. The answer given me was that when the railroad was pushing west, there was a typhoid epidemic and work stopped. By the time the disease subsided, a small city had grown up.

The theater had the rings of balconies usually associated with an opera house. We had a good crew made up of local stagehands and our own chiefs. In those days the stagehands' union was patriarchal, and membership was difficult to obtain for anyone not a son or relative of an established member. If you came across a good hand, you might ask, "Whose son is that?" If he was a lemon, you could ask, "Whose son-in-law is that?"

Some senior members of the union in New York held several well-paying jobs at once. They could work at a shop building scenery during the day, pull the curtain on Broadway that night, run across the street to a second job and shift a setting, run back for the next curtain, and so forth. (As we say, timing is everything.) Out-of-work stagehands could complain that a few hands were sucking up the available jobs, and they did complain, but to no avail during my time in New York.

The first opera we did in Indianapolis was LA BOHÈME, and I developed a way to shift in full sight from Act I, the garret, to Act II, the street café. We could also shift in sight from the Act III inn back to the Act I garret, and therefore have only one intermission, a good idea for a touring company. But José was not the boss in these matters. In opera, the conductor is supreme, and he vetoed the idea of only one intermission, pointing out that Puccini hadn't planned it that way.

José thrived in this work, more than in directing new plays. I do not believe that he was good at editing them. That was a fine skill of Arthur Penn, Tyrone Guthrie, and Elia Kazan. Some producers were also good at this: Kermit Bloomgarden, Cy Feuer, and Robert Whitehead.

José did not have to cut or edit operas. His work was inspiring the cast in other areas. He was dealing with trained singers who were not always good actors. He would tell them personal stories that could wring tears from stones — and brilliant acting from singers. One story I remember was that his father had a mistress, and everyone knew it. José, age ten, was playing outside one evening, and happened to look down a narrow street. Crossing the main avenue at the end of the street was a funeral procession: a tiny coffin on a flatbed funeral car, and walking behind it only one person, his father.

Again, news travels fast. In the big Indianapolis theater, when a scene being rehearsed became thrilling, the staff would gather: accountants and seamstresses from the third floor, the janitorial staff, everyone. José would have just told one of his stories and work would take flight. The problem was that the advances or breakthroughs in these rehearsals didn't always stick. When the initial emotion wore off, the cast rarely had enough acting technique to maintain the progress. Yet it was good work.

The next year, José directed Carlisle Floyd's SUSANNAH, and I designed it well enough. One problem was that Susannah has to be seen naked by the elders. Skin-colored tights and top are easy enough, and you want to believe she is naked, but not really. Five words of advice for a situation like this: upstage, back view, gauze, leaves. It worked, and we didn't get thrown out of Indianapolis.

That was the last season for the company. They needed money and the Reader's Digest Foundation offered it. Rudolph Bing, the general manager of the Met, turned it down. You can give it to the parent company, he said.

Bing ended up not liking Risë. It is sad to hold animosity toward someone you have appointed yourself. He also disliked opera in English, being of the school that wanted the original form, and he spoke French and Italian and German — or so I've been told. He spoke English to me when he looked at my sketches, indifferently. When he attended our English-language BOHÈME, he said that the only words he understood were in the stage manager's announcement. Sung English has a bad rap in opera, but in my experience the translations can be carefully constructed to be clear when sung. Listen to Marc Blitzstein.

Also, decided Bing, this business of spending diversionary time and money to develop singers isn't necessary; this is not a baseball farm team — we can audition young singers ourselves. Right? I don't know, but it was a shame to close the company.

Today, the Met has outreach through their simulcasts, and captioning solves the language gap. But I miss the youth and the fevered aspiration that Risë's company embodied. Toward the end of my thirty years directing the Theatre of the Deaf, it was that failure of desire among young potential actors that was disheartening. We had opened the job market for deaf people but, not having stage fever from childhood, they could now seek better-paying jobs and not live the gypsy life on the road.

WHAT I LEARNED

A note about captioning, which I mentioned. The National Theatre of the Deaf was involved at the beginning of its development for stage and television. It had existed for a long time in foreign film. When the company started, I went down to a captioning meeting in Washington, DC. Nanette Fabray, who had hearing problems, was involved as well. We discussed captioning for deaf people, and started a successful campaign advocating that all TV sets should have a line devoted to captioning, and make it available at the touch of a button. At a later hearing before a congressional committee, a congressman noted that he would never use that button, and a deaf person replied that she never used the sound button.

At our meeting, we outlined grandiose plans. We would not ask to caption ordinary stuff like *I Love Lucy*, but go for high-level culture: PBS offerings and the like. A deaf man, who had a high but clear voice, spoke up: "You don't understand. We don't need the 'high-falutin.' We just want the same shit everyone else has."

Concerning nudity onstage in SUSANNAH. At the Folies Bergère, partial nudity is an expected attraction. In HAIR or SIX DEGREES OF SEPARATION, full nudity moved us along. But it is an eye popper and brain grabber, and the mental typhoon in the middle of this opera might stop progress, might make the story jump out of the frame your mind has established. In such a situation you might give the audience comfort by indicating the nudity and at the same time adding clues that it is not real, only staged. Thus the flow of our famous "suspension of disbelief" moves along. Each situation is different. These were our thoughts for that opera.

EXERCISE

It has been said to me, and I believe it, that when there is group nudity onstage, as in HAIR, the men look at the men and the women look at the women. Is this true? Think about it.

CHAPTER TWENTY-NINE

My Sad Ending with José

D ESIGNERS, AS I'VE SAID, are not at the top of the food chain. Our design work is usually valued, but selling tickets is a complex equation. (Current exception, THE LION KING, where you do leave the theater whistling the sets and costumes.) There is a rigid social scale in New York (and elsewhere). Quintero commented that he received the greatest respect from his cast and others during rehearsals of LONG DAY'S JOURNEY, but actors take over when a play opens, and he sank a level in relation to Jason Robards and Fredric March, whose names were selling the tickets (added to O'Neill's, of course). When my son, Dan, and I wrote a book that was featured in the *New York Times Book Review,* notes from friends could be sorted into two piles. One was congratulatory and said that the sender was about to read the book. The other, also congratulatory, noted with ill-concealed intent and surprise that we had risen socially in the eyes of the sender and those others who counted.

José was concerned with being on Broadway, or more accurately, not being on Broadway. He'd been on top of the theater scene during LONG DAY'S JOURNEY, not only because of the success of the play, but because of the Eugene O'Neill revival. He moved to a lower Fifth Avenue penthouse, and there were constant parties. Leonora and I attended at least once a week, sensing that a refusal wouldn't be welcomed. We had a good time. José started to drink.

Fast forward: many productions, many years, a close friendship, and a fine working relationship. We sailed together; we met to just chat. Then he went to a sanatorium to dry out. He met an agent, in for the same purpose, and in that life-changing atmosphere, the agent pledged that he would devote the rest of his career exclusively to José. When they emerged, José was asked to direct a production of O'Neill's ANNA CHRISTIE with Liv Ullmann. He phoned me from California and outlined the project, and of course I was delighted. "But," said José, "my agent's companion will do the lighting." I said I understood and started to work. I tried, and tried again. I couldn't do it. If I were a costumer and was asked to design an outfit, but someone else would design the shoes and the handbag, I might have been as constipated — these accents can bring the whole scheme to life, or destroy it. In the forty-eight or so Broadway shows I had designed since Tharon had lighted LONG DAY'S JOURNEY, I had done my own lighting, perhaps the only set designer besides Jo Mielziner who was doing both jobs. After a week, I realized it was hopeless and phoned José. He said he understood. I did not say that the agent's companion was a notoriously poor lighting designer. That was not the problem; the problem was me.

At this time, I was starting the Theatre of the Deaf, and a few weeks later, I phoned José and asked if he would direct one of our first plays, a short play, part of an evening. He said he would talk to his agent, called back the next day, and said that his agent thought it a bad idea. "I've just come back on the scene," he said, "and to start out on a low-level project for the handicapped would reintroduce me on a lower level professionally."

I said that I believed the work would be beautiful and of high quality, and it could start a relationship between him and the company that could be nourishing and long-lasting. The phone almost jumped out of my hand, and these words I can quote exactly, because pain preserves memory: "How *dare* you, David, try to dazzle me with your little project!" *Slam*!

There it was. I believe José's reaction was not based so much in the perceived inferior level of my company as in my brazen effort to raise my position and be his boss.

Jason Robards and Colleen Dewhurst both worked for my company — or worked for *me*, as José might say. Jerry Robbins did not. I presented him with a short poetry section. "David, you just want to use my name to enhance something that doesn't really require hard work."

"You're right," I said, "but you understand how hard I'm trying to get away from 'help for the handicapped' to a professional sheen."

"Of course I understand," he said, and our relationship continued unharmed.

One way that we did give the company that sheen was to ask Al Hirschfeld to do our poster, and he did. We benefitted because anything Al inked became Broadway — or at least professional. Tyrone Guthrie agreed to work with us, and so did the fearless Joe Layton, who directed a sparkling GIANNI SCHICCHI.

My relationship with José staggered on a bit. Three years after that terrible phone call, the company was to film a Garcia Lorca piece for WGBH television. I thought this would attract José, and it did. He was paid part of his fee in advance, but he never showed up. A year later, he phoned and asked if I would meet him at an apartment he had been loaned at Des Artistes on West Sixty-Seventh Street. It was a beautiful space. José was broke and appreciated the kindness of the apartment's owner. His mother was dying, and he needed money to fly home to Panama. (She died about five times.) We chatted, but he could not resist telling me that I was "using his friends" for the company. He meant Colleen and Jason, whom I had met through him. More of the "who do you think you are" attitude. I wasn't disturbed — it wasn't that important — but I made a mistake. Unaware until it was too late, I looked up at the beautiful space. José caught the glance, and understood that I was thinking *he* was using his friends. He asked me to leave. End of story — but not of sadness. I was devoted to that man. He had entered hard times, and his own world was askew. He claimed that he understood my inability to work on ANNA CHRISTIE, but perhaps he felt I did not fully accept homosexual relationships, and that the web that held him with his agent's companion was too sticky for me.

WHAT I LEARNED

Theatre is as lively as I portray, and we take our lumps and get over them. But this sadness with José I have not gotten over. Who was foolish, who unfaithful? We both were, and we both lost. We connected; our minds worked well together; it was always fun. When, rarely, I did not design for him, we both saw that José did not have that mysterious connection with other designers — good, damn good, designers — but he did not pull out their best work as he did from me.

When I began the National Theatre of the Deaf, my Broadway designing slowed, then almost stopped. No producer wants another producer to look over his shoulder. I was now such a producer, however insane my project. And would you hire a designer who doesn't believe his profession is worthy enough, who wants to rise above it? That's how a producer might think. But some shows came to me, and, once I was in stride with my company, I was able to design scenery without designing the lighting. Necessity can turn you around.

EXERCISE

Think carefully about designing both settings and lighting. Add in costumes. When I studied, I thought of doing all, and I have some costume sketches from my London days that I believe are good. But times have changed. Despite the ease of computer control, lighting has become more technical. Sound, simple in my day, is an added specialty. In my case, the few costumes I designed in New York — off Broadway, and once for a ballet — were passable, but not good. Think about this, and make some choices. Perhaps, as in my case, they will be made for you.

CHAPTER THIRTY

Conceiving a Production

I REMEMBER Peter Blake's "Aha!" when he conceived the theater we were developing. A good exclamation to announce a concept. Perhaps "Eureka!" is better.

A concept is, to me, an enveloping idea that propels and unites a work (not necessarily a work of art). The Marshall Plan or a universal health-care plan can be called concepts. A concept can be short-term — just an idea to get something moving, what Alfred Hitchcock called "the McGuffin"— and may not endure to be apparent in the finished work. But it generates and unites ideas as the project begins.

I've described Peter Blake's concept. Here's another, a beautiful lighting job by Arden Fingerhut. She had been my student, and I'm proud of that. I asked her about her concept after seeing the performance. She said that she had noted the large French doors in the single-set living room, and thought that she should start each scene with a projection of the garden leaves, as if a streetlight beyond the garden threw their shadows into the room. The result was strong in one or two places, when the room was otherwise in darkness and the leaf patterns danced on the walls in shades of green or lavender. But usually it was subtle. "No matter if you didn't see it," she said. "The thought buoyed me, and united the whole progress of the work, and gave me a rounded sense of what I was doing."

Recently I designed a setting for a friend, Lary Bloom, at a local theater. The plot concerned a couple who are living together, but she is a prisoner to the memory of her husband, who vanished years ago in Vietnam. Killed? Missing and still alive? The play progresses in scenes alternating between the couple in the present and the soldier in his tent in the past. The woman

is haunted, unable to live fully because of her questions. I gave almost half
of the small stage to the soldier, and the other portion to the living room
of the battling couple. But the full background to both was the dense Viet-
namese forest, his locale and her overwhelming and dreadful memory.

Even smaller parts or details of a work can have their own concept to
organize them in your mind. What is a sculptor to do with hands? If you
look at Daniel Chester French's statue at the memorial in Washington,
notice that Lincoln's hands are loosely held in his initials, the letters *A* and
L in the sign-language alphabet. Really? I believe so. French had done a
statue at Gallaudet College (now Gallaudet University) for the deaf, and
knew this much sign language.

You can overdo concepts. We designers often visited each other during
load-ins, and we had little to do except sit in the back of the auditorium,
watch the crew unload crates, and gossip. One day there was Boris, with a
bad cold, looking like a pile of cow dung with a million green flies buzzing
about his head. "I just saw a film of MACBETH," he groaned. "Someone
thought 'leather,' and that's what you saw. Leather, leather, leather. I almost
got sick."

Soon after I built a small Japanese bath in our house and lined the walls
with redwood. Redwood, redwood, redwood! I started looking for boards
with serious flaws of color or grain to break the uniform quality of that
wood. I found some brass towel racks that interrupted and helped.

In NO STRINGS, we did not have the walls of a photo studio, but the
little trees and the spotlights we rolled around onstage would be appropriate props from the studio, as they served to make Paris avenues. They
grew out of their origins as studio props and depicted something else. This
is an aspect of "transformation," usually a good thing, even a necessary
ingredient, in our work.

Many concepts are poor. Someone says "Let's do it on a submarine!"
and that delights everyone until it opens. A concept should answer all the
questions. A good concept unties knots. If you tie yourself into knots to
support it, it's not good.

Opera work is a good format for these thoughts. We try to be clever
to show that an old show is still relevant. But any good show probably

is, and it might suffer more than it gains from a big concept. Is it worth the loss, say, of beautiful clothes and surroundings for LA TRAVIATA, replaced by today's sleek clothes and concrete? Sometimes supplying a bold new concept is damaging; it's just intellectual showing off. In a recent HANSEL AND GRETEL, there was no surrounding, mysterious forest. It was replaced by images of hunger, such as a greedy mouth painted on a backdrop. I understand someone's thought that this opera is about hunger, but it's also about abandonment and mystery and courage, and I want the threatening woods. The frightened children are lost in an enchanted forest; but here there was none. Hungry lips on the backdrop is an idea, an intellectual frolic, a printed sign onstage, not an engulfing mood. Is that the way you want to tell the story to your grandchildren? Would it even be remembered?

Another example: Gounod's FAUST is an old chestnut, and I understand that it has lost attendance. But I spent uncomfortable hours watching fine singers struggle against a flimsy idea. As in HANSEL AND GRETEL, the music was unchanged. But the backgrounds were of war scenes: not just one war, but two — both World War I and World War II. (Should I be flattered as a designer that scenery and costumes alone are sent into battle to sell an old work?) In this way, war was generalized — and yes, it is terrible; we live in a rotten world, and it all relates to the Devil himself, and the Devil relates to poor Marguerite. Dressing him in a bright blue, double-breasted, pin-striped suit is tempting, and I can hear, "Wow! Instead of a spinning wheel, we can seat Marguerite at a sewing machine! Our concept really works!" But do I need a projection of an atomic bomb exploding to deepen my connection to the misery of the young woman? Has today's world so passed by this old codger that the personal tragedy needs that kind of support? Saying that her distress is deepened in our minds by the immolation of Hiroshima trashes both. We need our Anne Frank to give us a bridge into the horror of the six million — but it doesn't work well the other way around. Today, abortions are available and children born out of wedlock don't raise an eyebrow. Therefore, I was left wondering why this suddenly modern Marguerite was suicidal at her dilemma. As an educated or intelligent man, I want to visit a past where an out-of-wedlock pregnancy was a calamitous happening, and inspired a great composer. Isn't that a reason to see classics — to understand our tortured history?

Read this wrenching poem by Walter Savage Landor, whose life over-lapped Gounod's in the mid-1800s:

Mother, I cannot mind my wheel;
My fingers ache, my mouth is dry;
O! if you felt the pain I feel!
But O, who ever felt as I?

No longer could I doubt him true —
All other men may use deceit;
He always said my eyes were blue,
And often swore my lips were sweet.

WHAT I LEARNED

Sometimes a fresh concept, even a veneer, can be exciting and valid. But I'm suspicious when it falls on designers, when only the set and costumes are changed. But one production I remember worked well, a LOVE'S LABOUR'S LOST at the Brattle, conceived by Albie Marre and Richard Baldridge. With its costumes and sets of the Edwardian era, designed beautifully by Robert O'Hearn and Robert Fletcher, we enjoyed a whiff of late-Victorian morality, familiar to us, and that helped illuminate the play.

Or, you can redo the whole production and give us another WEST SIDE STORY. What works, works. Don't let my rant discourage you from taking risks. Do not be frantic if your props or scenery are not absolutely accurate. You will be called out for errors: "That kind of pistol wasn't invented until a year after your show takes place," says a firearms expert. Some people sadly reason, "Gosh, if the audience is worried about *that,* the show's no good anyway. So never mind some stupid pistol." Wrong. This is a misera-ble justification for sloppy work.

This introduces a small dilemma and subtle choices. In my home, I have furniture designed and built last year side by side with furniture designed and built two hundred and fifty years ago. So, if I design an English parlor of 1690, are all the furnishings on-the-dot contemporary, or does the room display the same variety as my own home? The latter would probably be the case. But it is important to establish the time of the play with as many tools as possible and to exclude confusion. It can also be telling to furnish the room by emphasizing the culmination of the time that preceded it. Perhaps ancestral portraits from a former age? Or two contrasting settings, as in Vanbrugh's THE RELAPSE? All this is not easy to do, and perhaps could be confusing to the nonexpert eye. How many expert eyes are there, anyway, like Pat or Fred, who knew when the buttonhole style changed on the Pope's robes? My advice: be an expert. But if you are not, be critical, but just a little forgiving.

EXERCISE

You will be called upon again and again when you design to come up with a concept. Perhaps not by the director or producer, but always by yourself. Perhaps a concept is a motivator, not appearing by itself in the finished product the way mine appeared in the Vietnam play. Flex your imagination in these directions. When you read any book, set it or parts of it in your mind. How would you set a certain scene — or, yes, enhance it? Remember Kazan's thought for THE NIGHT CIRCUS. What is important for that foredeck in MOBY DICK? For one of Hercule Poirot's revelations?

CHAPTER THIRTY-ONE

Violetta and the Parade

I'VE NOT designed Verdi's LA TRAVIATA, but I've seen fine versions, live and on film. They bring a curious thought to me, and if I were to design this opera I would want to resolve it when I started work. Odd, to start my thinking about the end of the opera, not at its beginning. Or you can say that you start with the whole work, but are intrigued to solve a particular detail, and the solution could invigorate your thinking.

In Act III, which our beloved Violetta uses up by dying, a parade passes outside her bedroom window. This brief interlude contrasts with the somber scene. The joyful music tells us that life goes on after death; it is a celebration of life as she is losing hers, an additional agony to the dying woman and her fans in the audience. In one version, we see, through cloudy windows, the masquers energetically marching and dancing. A corny idea? Perhaps. But bring on corny ideas! Sentimental too, but by then we are weeping anyway. My point is that I would have preferred to not see the marchers. The parade is mentioned, and we know what makes the outside noise because Violetta asks her maid, who explains that it is carnival, and Paris is going wild with pleasure. I would have placed the apartment on a higher floor, or placed the windows high, to prevent direct street-level vision. The windows are important because of the daylight coming into the room, adding an adjustable element in the drama, but to me seeing the parade outside is too much. Let our inner vision imagine the scene; let's stay with our ears. Is this strange that a designer wants to see less? The parade idea is wonderful musically, but to me the image of revelers overplays the moment, and what the music conveys is reduced. It takes us away from inner emotion to an external scene — curiously, seeing the external scene distracts from the very emotion that it caused. The pain of that joyous music when Violetta is dying makes me want to shut my eyes and cover them with my hands. But there are other approaches. Do we see the parade while Violetta does not? Or perhaps upon hearing the music, Violetta staggers to the curtained window and tears down the drapes. She watches the joyful scene for only a second, then falls back, exhausted, onto the bed. Melodramatic? Yes. A problem here is that we are now left with the bare window. Perhaps the maid, prompted by her mistress's distress, would quickly cover it with a light folding screen, common in those rooms. The joyful scene, then a deliberate act to conceal it — a whole new mini-scene. The director will make this decision. Perhaps the musical director will veto it. Ideally, we will all make it together.

WHAT I LEARNED

Beware of clever concepts to bring a production "up to date." Interesting thinking, but before you leap, compare it to the author's intent. It may be more compelling to understand the story as written.

Here's a bold statement from Roger Furse, who pushed me along on this journey. (It's not his original thought; I believe it was stated by V. S. Pritchett, a British writer best known for fine short stories.) Roger said, "Nothing is real, nothing is understood, until the artist explains it to us." Gosh, is that really true? But we shouldn't give such statements a rigorous and stifling truth test. Instead, we should welcome whatever stimulates our thinking. Try to apply this whopper in a modest way; take a baby step. Look for an hour at some of Monet's haystacks, and I guarantee you'll never again see a haystack the same way. Proceeding from there, the audacious thought becomes more interesting.

Speaking of opera, I think of my first teacher, Robert O'Hearn, who designed fine settings at the Met for DER ROSENKAVALIER and DIE FRAU OHNE SCHATTEN. The latter is about a woman without a shadow. Pay attention to shadows, I learned — they can be expressive. When you are focusing a lamp, the pattern on the stage floor shows the center of the light and the spread of the light, with your head's shadow in the middle. And you can color shadows onstage — did you know that?

I particularly watch shadows when I'm driving, because they tell me where the sun is, and therefore I sense "north." On clear days, I navigate my car journeys by the sun. I'm often lost. I could listen to that lady on my phone who tells me when to turn. But I have keen memories of navigating by sun and moon and stars at sea. It's all magic. Yes, it's all explainable — but it's still magic.

EXERCISE

Is your computerized world just complex technology? What is magical? Did you understand the world as magical when you were a child? What magic have we lost in this technological age?

Perhaps even a good concept is a form of magic. Think this through — or not, because it's the hardest exercise in this book.

CHAPTER THIRTY-TWO

First Steps into Another World

A T GREEN MANSIONS, my first real job, and where I met Leonora, dance teams such as Marge and Gower Champion showed up for a weekly dance night. Other guests came by. I can never forget Evan Long singing, with a few dance steps, "It Ain't Necessarily So."

Leonora knew many such entertainers, and she had been a favorite of Agnes de Mille and Alwin Nikolai. Three years after we moved to New York, Todd Bolender, who had choreographed STILL POINT and SOU-VENIRS for the New York City Ballet, phoned. He was choreographing THE MASQUERS, and he had been given my name — would I design it? Of course. Sets and costumes. It didn't turn out well — his work or mine. Despite generous help from Madam Karinska's workshop, my clothes were mediocre. The set was so-so; the dance was no better. Not Todd's best. Fortunately, Lincoln Kirstein, producer of the company, gave me a second chance, and I designed Frank Moncion's PASTORALE. This is the story of a blind man, resting alone in a grove of trees, who becomes involved with young picnickers. When they leave, he is left alone again, and Frank made that into a touching loneliness. Ruth Sobotka, one of the loveliest of his dancers, designed the beautiful clothes. Two years later she committed suicide. I do not know why. Lincoln said to me that a person who commits suicide is trying to destroy two people.

The set was a grove of birch trees. Its gossamer patches of leaves were made of wire mesh sprayed with cobwebs and painted in various shades of gold, brass, bronze, and a metallic green. Jean Rosenthal lit it well. When the young dancers leave, the blind man sorrowfully turns and goes slowly back into the grove. We developed a cue of intense white light on the grove against a sky that turned from blue to black. The picture was like an afterimage — what you might see after looking into a bright light and then closing your eyes, an interior image on the back of your eyelids — a comment on what a blind man might "see." This was powerful.

I had met Lincoln Kirstein during my last year of college. I came to New York and asked him questions about designers. My thesis concerned easel painters who had become set designers, willingly or not, or whose works had been adapted to sets: Christian Bérard, Marc Chagall, Georges Rouault, Raoul Dufy, and Eugene Berman. (I should have included Picasso.) Later, I was to retouch the backdrops of all these men except Bérard, and I met Berman when I was helping to paint his DON GIOVANNI at the Met. He had devised a large cartouche on one of the drops and put his initials in it. Rudolph Bing was angry, and said that Berman could use "WAM," Mozart's initials, but not his own.

Lincoln was gracious to me. He liked my college thesis when it was completed, and had it printed in a small arts magazine he had founded. I doubt that he had anything to do with my start for the New York City Ballet — that came about through Leonora. But Lincoln liked me and my work for many years, before the inevitable explosion, when I was booted out like the sorcerer's apprentice, following the traditional trajectory of every designer who had ever worked for Lincoln.

Lincoln was an imposing figure, tall and big (not fat), with a granite face and an eagle glance under a crew cut. He wore boldly black clothes. He had been General Patton's driver in the Second World War, he told me. He was volatile, and at times you trod on eggshells in a conversation. At other times, you were his best buddy. He was fond of Leonora, and we cared for him. The ballet company was thought of as Balanchine's, but most of us who were involved saw Lincoln's enormous intelligence and devotion, and we understood it was his as well. He enjoyed watching male dancers, which helped balance Balanchine's devotion to women.

Not many understood that Lincoln, not Balanchine, was responsible for the scenic "look" of the New York City Ballet. Lincoln usually determined if there should be any set at all. Then the early morning phone calls

Opening night of A MIDSUMMER NIGHT'S DREAM, with (*left to right*) author;
Robert Irving, musical director; Mr. B.; and Madam Karinska.
Photographer: Martha Swope. Author's collection.

(Lincoln was an insomniac): "David, get down here, George is starting a
new ballet."

Madam Karinska held sway in the kingdom of costumes. Unless Mr. B.
specified that he wanted only that simplest leotard look, she produced
the beautiful clothes that in many ways distinguished the company. (We
all called Balanchine "Mr. B.," except Lincoln, who called him George. I
called him George rarely, and it made me uncomfortable.)

Lincoln and his wife, Fidelma, had a home near Gramercy Park — a
carriage house, two floors filling most of the depth of the hundred-foot
plot. The interior was handsomely decorated — a gold room to the right as
you went in, for instance — but its appeal was in the long hallway crammed

with treasures. There were well-framed paintings, some by Fidelma's brother, Paul Cadmus; some of Fidelma's own amateur but skillful work. There were portraits of Lincoln, some nude, and all interesting. There were also shelves of precious toys and odd sculptures from people at the ends of the earth. This hallway led to a comfortable room with a fireplace, facing the small back garden. Lincoln burned aromatic hickory in the fireplace. I sometimes smell that rare wood today, and it is a reminder of this giant of a man. After he threw me out of the ballet, I met him and told him how grateful I was to him. Then he would phone me once a year, complain that he was getting old, and make a handsome donation to my Company. Once he asked Leonora and me to come to his house because he was auditioning a puppet master. The small stage was set up in the gold room, with three delicate gilded ballroom chairs facing it. The show began, and Lincoln immediately fell asleep. I held him by the elbow, carefully adjusting the pressure, because I did not want him to snore, and I was fearful of waking him suddenly, when he would sometimes leap and shout. (I'd been through that many times during ballet rehearsals.) When the puppet show ended, Lincoln woke and gave a long, relevant, and brilliant criticism.

At our early morning meetings at Lincoln's house, we were often joined by Eddie Bigelow, assistant manager of the ballet. I sailed with Eddie in a small boat from Africa to West Seventy-Ninth Street in 1963. We would go to the breakfast room just off the back parlor, and Fidelma ("Fido") would produce breakfast. The dialogue between her and Lincoln about the darkness of the toast, when or if the coffee was ready, and so forth, put Eddie and me in a mad tea party, holding back our laughter. Then the intense work would start. The rooms downstairs were jammed with books, but there apparently was a library room upstairs. I imagine it so full that I see metal shelving. Lincoln would dash up and return carrying fabulous books with hand-painted illustrations from the eighteenth or nineteenth centuries — how he conceived it should look — or show us the work of an artist who should be studied before putting brush to paper. Then he would not refer to this again. He never said, for example, "David, I thought we decided to use images from Piranesi for this." This was because once Lincoln's usually brilliant conception was stated, he respected his artists;

he didn't crowd them the way Bill Ball did. When the work was being assembled onstage, however, he was a poor critic: once he came to me and said that he thought a certain orange was too bright. He was pointing at a ladder I was holding for an electrician. I didn't know if he was serious, but Balanchine, who overheard this, believed he was. For years, when we were setting up, Mr. B. would point to any old thing, such as a tattered brown sweater hanging in the wings, and say, "David, didn't we agree on yellow?"

Lincoln regained perspective when the show opened, and he would make encouraging statements such as, "You've caught the scale of this huge theater!" He never said that my work on such and such was mediocre, though it sometimes was.

We often worked too fast and with too little money. Sometimes this succeeded. One Thursday, Lincoln came to my house and said that there was a new dance opening Tuesday, and George had not asked for a set but maybe it would be a good thing — it was George's birthday, and this would be Lincoln's gift. The ballet was called NATIVE DANCERS, about jockeys and horses. I ran around Friday and found pleasant translucent cloth of the right width (no sewing needed), and on Monday, Chester Rakeman made the kind of white railing that edges racecourses, and a batten. All we had to do was space out and drape and staple the cloth strips on that batten, then carry them forward to attach to an overhead pipe downstage, and there we had an airy, full-stage canopy, and a fence for dancers to lounge on when not in midair. We rigged this Tuesday morning. Mr. B. saw it at Tuesday afternoon's dress rehearsal. And he liked it, and praised me — and Lincoln.

WHAT I LEARNED

Work at the ballet was never again as fast as for NATIVE DANCERS, but sometimes it was bewildering. For EPISODES, we had only a few days before rehearsals when — and this was rare Mr. B. — came to me directly. "David, I have for you no score, and piano will not convey it well." (He played expertly, if the keys were clean — one cannot play on dusty keys, he said.) "I also have not yet the dance fully in my head. But — do what you do." That was all he said. So I did what I did, and he liked it. In any collaboration, there's an exciting element of mind reading, and I remember this moment as the high point of all my work as a designer. Think of this: if you believe theatre design is a worthy craft, and then believe that working for Balanchine is the best there is, then these four words of trust and partnership are the pinnacle.

Martha Graham and company were to dance within EPISODES, and she knew exactly what she wanted and showed me a sketch. I did that. Three years later, she phoned and wanted me to redo the dance for a tour. She had new ideas — some musical changes, some choreographic changes. "No set changes? Martha, I have some new ideas, and it can be better. It's no longer in the surround of EPISODES, and should be changed." She said no, she wanted the same set, and so I asked to be excused. She understood. If I have a tombstone, it should read, "This man refused to work for Martha Graham!"

EXERCISE

Another drawing exercise: Using paper and pencil or marker, draw anything you want, even from memory — but once started, do not lift the pencil or marker from the paper. Make a continuous line drawing. With luck the main image will be so strong that the crossover continuous lines will not detract. They may add vitality.

CHAPTER THIRTY-THREE

More Ballet

I DON'T REGRET the hasty work I did for the ballet. I would take a new scheme to our manager, Betty Cage, and she would give me a budget and I would hold to it. Thus I became the cheap "ham sandwich." When we moved to Lincoln Center, a bit of caviar could be afforded, and I was not thought of as often. But I believe I had the best years. The work may have been low budget, but with more experimentation and less pressure than in later years, when it was felt necessary to answer Lincoln Center's demand to be monumental.

In those early years with the ballet, my apartment and studio were in Carnegie Hall, and its stage door, on the north side of Fifty-Sixth Street, was opposite City Center's stage door on the south side of Fifty-Sixth Street. The shortcut to my studio from City Center was through Carnegie Hall's stage door, followed by a sharp right into the basement, and finally up a short flight of stairs to the elevator. But — one of the amusements of those early years — en route, you had to step through a giant fan belt that ran the air-conditioning. The big wheel was about six feet in diameter, and perhaps eight feet away, the belt circled the smaller wheel, about two feet in diameter. The thick rubber belt whirred powerfully around these wheels, and it was foolish to stoop and step through — but it was fun. And we were like kids in such matters. (But I would have felt bad if Mr. B. or Lincoln had been ground up.)

In the late fifties, the great Carnegie Hall was to be torn down and replaced with a red skyscraper. The evictors came by, but we thought it a shame to go. A small group of us, two other families and Luthier Rosenthal, who had his shop in the building, went to court. Because of a technicality concerning the parking lot, we won a stay. It was during this stay that Isaac Stern became involved, and, with others, saved the magnificent building where Tchaikovsky had conducted, and where, of more importance to me, I heard Jascha Heifetz from the first row. That was a life-changer to a teenage boy. We did eventually move out of Carnegie Hall. Leonora loved the old building, and more than once she crept downstairs to hear late night practicing, including a session with Van Cliburn. Some of her ashes are preserved in the hall, not just scattered to be devoured by vacuums but — I won't tell.

I met Jerry Robbins during my time at the ballet, when I spent my spare time backstage touching up the toys for Horace Armistead's THE NUT-CRACKER or any other useful thing I could do for this company that had become a family to me. I never designed for Jerry, but almost every year he had a new project, and he would phone, and I would meet him at his house or at the theater he would soon inhabit. He wanted to know what I thought about such and such a play, which he would describe if I had not read it. I did not make the awful mistake I had made with Garson Kanin — no, these were works not yet assigned to designers. There were always three or four other designers called to have these conversations. We all caught on because designers gossiped when we met at the shops or load-ins. Yes, we were auditioning for Jerry — but nothing was drawn on paper, which is the line we didn't cross. One of the reasons for the formation of our union was to defend against an old-time producers' game of getting this kind of information and ideas from good designers, and then hiring draftsmen or the cheapest people available to carry them out. We didn't feel that way with Jerry, though; sessions with this genius were fun and within our rules. We even thought of having a party of his "consultants" and inviting him.

Now a comment on lighting for this ballet company. When we work with a repertory system, we cannot refocus a multitude of instruments for every opera or ballet. There are units that work for everything: a cool wash over the entire stage, for example. Between ballets — and there might be four different dances in one night — a limited number of adjustments can be made. A few lamps within reach can be refocused; the plastic color "gels" that are in holders in front of the lenses can be changed — if they are within reach from the floor or a step-ladder, or even by skillful maneuvering of a long pole with a hook on its end to snatch off the gel from its holder and replace it. A limited number of "specials" are also available — lighting units for a certain purpose, such as a light to pick up the somnambulist when she mounts the stairs to her high room in the castle. Some lights can be refocused between evenings. If you are lucky, you have enough extra units — and spaces for them on the pipes overhead or the side booms — and don't have to refocus many. New remotely controlled lamps solve some of this. But it all requires meticulous planning: you are dealing with over five hundred units.

"Is ballet different than opera or Broadway?" my students ask, The centers of gravity of the stages are different, and you sense this as you are designing. Broadway usually sits comfortably onstage. There is a quality of height in opera — you don't squash the rising music with a low proscenium or a ceiling. Often you need levels (platforms) to accommodate a large chorus. In ballet, the dancers themselves float, or should seem to. I often felt I was addressing a sense of space that was not floor-based but air-based. My eye always felt lifted, somehow floating, when I saw the space in my imagination.

One attraction to opera designing is that you can underlight the sets. Spotlights pick out the singing performers, and the scenery can handsomely take color and shadow without the floor bounce that flattens it. All of this, again, is getting easier as we develop remotely controlled spotlights that can be directed, dimmed, and re-colored without needing a bulky space-devouring platform for the operator.

During the sixties, lighting designers began asking for box booms to be installed when we undertook a show. I believe that Tharon and I had the most success with this request. She would phone — "I've got one, David!" These box booms are the lights mounted on upright pipes (booms) that you see in the near-stage audience boxes of auditoriums. They get a good side angle on a performer, and they are not overly intrusive to a traditionally designed auditorium. Some theaters have gone farther, however, and you will see ugly pipes or grids of lights hung mid-ceiling, changing a graceful domed auditorium into something that feels like a factory.

If the theater you're working in has a second balcony, instruments mounted on its front may also have that good angle. The flat-on shot from the front of a low balcony will cast light, wanted or not, on your background. That can be great to smash in for a musical lineup, and with luck the scenic backdrop has been designed so it won't suffer from the cast's shadows.

WHAT I LEARNED

Jerry Robbins told me (and surely others) that he had been upset at how demanding and how cruel he was to his dancers during rehearsals. "But after four years on the couch," he said, "I am no longer upset."

From all of this I learned something that I used poorly. What would be the season's first evening presentation by the National Theatre of the Deaf? There are so many styles of work we could do to demonstrate our ability and flexibility. So why not do four contrasting short pieces, the way the ballet often did? It worked the first year. But the second year, when, like the ballet, we added two new short pieces but kept two old ones, people who saw us again objected. Why? They never objected when they saw SWAN LAKE Act I as the ballet closer night after night. The reason, I believe, is music. Sure, the Tchaikovsky is the same dance repeated, but the dance is cloaked in and rises from the music, and music can be heard again and again. That's the point. Our words — visual words, but spoken also — were nevertheless words, and were boring the second time around. Those years at the ballet I remember as musical years, more than as stick-and-canvas years. Now, in memory, I think of having had a career in music.

We did revive a few plays during my years with the National Theatre of the Deaf. They were not as good as they were the first time. To repeat Tchelitchew's advice, the dream is as good as the reality; don't destroy the remembered dream by making it a copied reality in the present. Why were these revivals for my theatre not as good? Didn't we learn, and improve with knowledge from our past mistakes? No. When I am stumped, I have a coffee with J Ranelli, who directed many works for us, and he explains. To paraphrase his take on this: when you do a show again, you are aware of the mistakes you made the first time, you focus on them, and you lose perspective on the show as a whole. You lose the energy of experimentation and risk. Your wingspan shortens. The moral, to me: keep your mistakes fresh.

A good question I've been asked concerning the scenery for the National Theatre of the Deaf is, how different is it to conceive scenery that will tour in a twelve-foot truck and set up in two hours, compared to scenery for Broadway that merits six end-loading balloon box cars? The curious answer is: not much. At least, not much different as we talk about conception and concept, not bulk or construction or set-up time. The question remains, what will enhance the play? A concept should emerge — and if it's solid, executing it is a series of steps that are often the same regardless of scale. For instance, the idea of a honeymoon for Scarlett and Rhett on a Mississippi riverboat might be discarded because the riverboat would become so small on our touring stage that it would be a mere street sign, an *indication,* and not an enveloping locale. That brings up the thought that possibly our theatre should not attempt the full GONE WITH THE WIND.

Trust your audience to "get it." In our set for GIANNI SCHICCHI, the effort and focus was on the great bed. The bed told us all: style of the period, wealth of the room, and so forth. We did not throw up a surround of the glorious city of Florence, or even of the ancient room that contained the bed. It worked. Of course, at the Met, a grand surround would be expected. (Expectations!) There, a bed alone would be shabby.

EXERCISE

Time for another drawing exercise. Draw an object or, better, the nude human form. (Go to a "life class.") Then redraw, but not the outline of the figure or object. Instead draw the "inline" of the space that the object interrupts. In theory, the resulting two drawings are the same, but the difference in approaches is instructive.

CHAPTER THIRTY-FOUR

The Grand Kabuki

L INCOLN BECAME ENAMORED with Japan. He brought over the Imperial Household Dancers, who danced an ancient form called gagaku. They used a platform about thirty inches high and twenty feet square. They wore beautiful costumes, entered ceremoniously, and stamped a lot. From consulting many sources, I was able to re-create the platform, and Willy Nolan's shop built it well, with turned "brass" finials (they were wood, but looked fine in their painted jackets). Lincoln wanted the dancers to wear a special costume to identify them as they strolled about New York City in 1960. They agreed, and the company of a dozen dancers and musicians arrived wearing identical blue pin-striped suits. They liked the look of my set, but complained — politely — that the platform didn't resist their stamping as firmly as the one at home.

Then some of us went to Japan. In the group with Lincoln were architect Philip Johnson and Bert Martinson (of coffee fame), who were Lincoln's friends, plus Eddie Bigelow and me. I arrived two days late, after a long flight. This was before jets, and the Starliner needed about sixteen hours to cross the Pacific after a stop in Alaska. I showed up at Frank Lloyd Wright's old Imperial Hotel at breakfast time. Lincoln looked up from his steak and eggs. "David! What are you doing here?"

". . . Betty Cage sent me," I managed.

Lincoln, sometimes forgetful, had asked for me, because the mission was to bring the Grand Kabuki to the states and there were technical questions such as boxcar size, flame-proofing, local crew support, and so on.

The negotiations, only a day old, had broken down. (It's true that you should never take yes for an answer in Japan.) So we were all shipped to Kyoto while things cooled down, and were at leisure in the old city. One quote I remember from Philip Johnson is this: "I don't mind eating raw things, but I hate it when they crawl across my plate in an attempt to get away specifically from *me*."

When things straightened out, we went back to Tokyo, and I met members of the family that had designed for Kabuki for four centuries. There was no uncertainty, no need for other authorities to check up on their opinions. They were surprisingly flexible: to some of my questions they might answer, "Yes, it was that way, but we changed it in the mid-1600s, and you could do it either way." One problem for me was that our stages are usually designed so tightly that from the balconies the sight lines permit you to see the conductor if there is a pit, or the front edge (apron) of the stage if the theater is small and not a musical house. To see more of the auditorium would create steeper angles in the balconies, or they would need to be farther away from the stage. In Kabuki, the *hanamichi*, the "flowerway," is a through-audience runway used for those long ceremonial entrances and exits. So how to make the *hanamichi* visible? Well, they could be at the sides — or anywhere at all, said the Japanese designers.

Eddie and I were invited to the Imperial Palace to see the original gagaku stage in one of its great rooms. The dancers, old-fashioned men who bowed and hissed, were there to greet us. (This was still, in 1960, old Japan, when men wore kimonos to business; when Tokyo, not yet rebuilt, was still lined with those wooden buildings that had not burned.) I was asked to go onto the gagaku stage, and I took off my shoes and did that. "See," said one dancer, jumping up and down, "see how sturdy it is. So much more solid than yours."

"True," I said, "but can you take it apart in six minutes and roll it out that door?"

"Ah!" said the dancers, and bowed and hissed and smiled, and took us to a lunch skillfully served by two elderly and homely geishas.

WHAT I LEARNED

When I was Roger Furse's apprentice, he showed me a newspaper article about a play he was doing. "Notice, David, how many of the facts are wrong. And yet every day, we read articles about other people and events, and assume the facts are right!" Here is an example of this important notion: In the *New York Times* magazine there was, back in the fifties and sixties, a column that, every week, put forth some question, such as "Where were you twenty-five years ago when this or that happened?" One week, they asked famous artists to name their favorite work of art. Martha Graham and Pablo Picasso were questioned; she mentioned a dance, and he mentioned a painting. Philip Johnson had wriggled into that crowd, and he answered that the fifteen-stone garden at the Ryoanji Temple in Kyoto was a work that "stunned one to silence." I was there, and here is what happened: after a few minutes, Bert Martinson turned and said, "Philip, can't you keep your fucking mouth shut for one goddamned minute?"

From the solidity — or not — of my gagaku platform, I learned again how thoughtful one must be concerning another person's apparent failure. The dancers disliked my work, but they were polite, and eventually understood the problem.

In Kyoto I learned — or at least experienced — what it is like to live in a work of art. I lived on a mat floor with paper doors, and breakfast was delivered by a woman who slid back the doors and moved through the doorway on her knees. Outside, you find yourself moving slowly, placing your feet carefully, and pausing every few feet to look around. True, you might still stop at McDonald's for lunch. Yet everything I designed after that week reached back, however unconsciously, to those spaces. Can it be different for any aware person? I have no doubt that my best (or favorite) set, for BUGAKU (not gagaku), came from walks in the old city. Those walks helped me extend and transform my thoughts about that old platform. The word that pops up again and again is "transformation."

EXERCISE

Here's a game I often play: imagination in transformation. What would it take, in costume and makeup, to change my sister-in-law into the witch in HANSEL AND GRETEL? To change that tree in my yard to an evil, grasping tree in Snow White's forest? Or my cat to the brilliant and resourceful Puss in Boots?

CHAPTER THIRTY-FIVE

Japan Again

M
Y EXPERIENCES with Japan did not stop for me. That visit was the first of a dozen, but subsequent trips were no longer for the ballet. Ten years later, Joe Layton asked me to design a musical version of *Gone with the Wind,* renamed SCARLETT, to be premiered in Japan — in Japanese. The production company Toho had the Japanese rights, and they had done SCARLETT as a play in two parts on two separate evenings. Now the next step: a musical in one evening. Harold Rome was the composer, and the book and lyrics were by Kazuo Kikuta. American musicals had toured in Japan, but this was the first of that genre to be created there.

One day I met the "fire and explosion expert" who was to arrange the burning of Atlanta. He was a small man, and I don't remember his features because his entire head, minus a peephole for one eye, was swathed in bandages.

The technical meetings for this production were endless, with populous attendance because no one wanted to be blamed, or so it seemed. Everyone had a specific job: one man was head of screws, another in charge of nails, and so forth. They were skillful and articulate. We allotted time for the building and painting and set-up. One drop was to be cut up as lace, with thousands of holes, but the crew said they would cut it during set-up. "It will take days," I said. "No, trust us"— and on set-up day, twenty men with scissors stood side by side and cut the holes as the drop was slowly raised into place. At home, we would not have the twenty hands, but if we did, they would have cut off neighboring ears and noses. In Japan, people were used to living and working in cramped spaces.

Instead of spending their honeymoon in London, I proposed that Scarlett and Rhett take their trip on a Mississippi riverboat, and Joe liked that.
The elegant two-storied boat appeared turning and rising in mist on the
huge turntable elevator of the Imperial Theater. Another good effect was
to put the long train bearing the wounded into Atlanta on the *hanamichi*,
running along the side of the auditorium, but visible to all. The train was
a hundred feet long.

The horse pulling the wagon that carried Scarlett and Rhett and the
pregnant Melanie out of Atlanta during the fire was the only veteran of
the dramatic versions of the play. He or she walked on a treadmill. Hidden
under the front seat of the wagon, a small horse-smart stagehand waited,
bamboo pole with dustpan attached at the ready. When the horse swished
its tail in a telltale way, the pole and pan shot out and caught the drop-
pings. This was so quickly and skillfully done that it was unseen by most.
When the show travelled to London, such a man and device were not used,
and this caused a long and raucous interruption just before our Act I finale.
The pile must have been a foot high.

In Tokyo, our Scarlett was well known nationally as the star of the Ta-
karazuka Kabuki theater in Hankyu, near Osaka. As we had often done in
the States, amusements were built at the ends of new rail lines to encourage
patronage. In the case of Hankya, a fine theater had been built. One feature of the theater was that the traditional all-male form, where men play
women, was reversed, and women played men.

At one moment in the show, Joe wanted his dancers to enter and, as
they formed a circle, plant small Confederate flags, then dance in and out
between them. Obviously the flags, knee high, would have to stand up.
They didn't. Half fell over most of the time. I went back to my "six mat"
hotel room, sat on the floor, and determined not to sleep until I had solved
this. One easy solution is to have the small flagpoles rise from a dumbbell,
but I had wanted flat bases, and those were already built. I woke in the
morning with the idea. The six-inch square bases of the flags were heavy
enough, but the flags were top-heavy and the props tipped over unless me-
ticulously placed. There was no time for such care by the running dancers. The answer? Saw through the flagpole two inches above the base and

secure a small spring connecting the base and the flagpole. The spring was weak and the weight of the pole and flag would not influence the base as it set down — the leverage would be lost because the top-heavy pole and flag just flopped over. But when the base settled, the spring was strong enough to bring the pole and its flag up to vertical. Designers are not rocket engineers, but I solved that problem, and I've solved other such problems with pleasure.

When SCARLETT opened at the Drury Lane in London it was not as good as it had been in Japan. That happens: the good cuts don't happen; the director tries to make it more low-brow — or too elegant — good actions are forgotten; the cast is not as fervent. On the good side, it was shorter. Rome and Kikuta could take out the honorifics — the elaborate, formal terms of address between the Japanese characters were dropped. About ten minutes of the show vanished.

My work on this musical in Japan created friendships that brought the Theatre of the Deaf twice to Japan, and that is when I experienced the memorable moment in Hiroshima that I've mentioned earlier. We brought two Japanese actors into our company for a time, and when they returned to Japan, they established a Theatre of the Deaf in Japan, under the leadership of Tetsuko Kuroyanagi.

WHAT I LEARNED

The Imperial Theater in Tokyo was a big theater with an operatic-size stage, a full-stage turntable elevator, and the like. During these years, I learned about scale. Recall Lincoln's remark that I had found the scale of the big New York State Theater. That was for Jacques d'Amboise's IRISH FANTASY. We had a huge green curtain downstage, covering the entire proscenium, about sixty feet wide and forty feet high. It was made of see-through lace — Irish lace — and a short prologue to the ballet was seen through it, mistily, as I had hoped. Then the bottom of the curtain was fetched back and up while the front and top of it stayed put, and it became a ceiling to the ballet.

More fascinating to me, and harder to learn, but a part of my job, was the scale of emotions. So here are more thoughts from our large-scale emotional effort: opera.

The Met has done an inventive and beautiful MADAME BUTTERFLY. For me, it is damaged (not ruined) by the final moments. Butterfly tugs at our hearts not because she is a monumental character but because her life is so modest — similar to Mimi in LA BOHÈME. A great character can have a great death, but beware of an effort to magnify a player whose essence is not heroic but modest, particularly if that's why we love her. It emphasizes how much all lives matter —"art" makes us understand this. Is this really a design function? Yes: center stage placement, lighting, and costuming all come together to create the heroic picture of Butterfly's death that I'm questioning.

Violetta is different. She was a socialite, so to speak, and her death is a sad retribution for the sinful life she struggled to escape. We become involved in her struggle. We want her life to change, to be saved, through her love.

But with the gentle Butterfly, an innocent young woman who was abandoned, we are heartbroken that her simple trust is so cruelly abused and her great possession, her baby son, is taken from her. Her death, heroically and grandly staged stage center, harmed the pity and dried my tears. As for Mimi's gentle death in LA BOHÈME, again, does this have anything to do with sets, with stage position and furniture and lighting? Of course it does. José, in our production for the Met's second company, wanted Mimi to die in a chair: she was not even granted the comfort of a bed. The chair was not stage center. It worked.

EXERCISE

Recently I saw a dreadful event in a restaurant. A family was celebrating, balloons and all, a somewhat bewildered boy, no more than five years old, who was dressed in full academic regalia: the familiar gown, the mortarboard headgear. He was being honored for his graduation from kindergarten. I'm sure he was given a diploma, which he couldn't read. Thus our meaningful ceremonies are trashed.

Overdo this: Invent *new* ceremonies. Invent the regalia, a grand flight of steps or a pedestal, a surrounding golden-tasseled tent, for a successful filling at the dentist's. Or imagine a golden coach drawn by six white horses entering a stadium on a blood-red carpet, a girl waving and all standing and cheering to celebrate: she has been touched by the magic wand of the fairy of menarche. Perhaps that fairy has her own float or coach. Nautch girls could sway at the corners of the carpet.

CHAPTER THIRTY-SIX

Turntables and Puppets

....

HE RIVERBOAT rising on a huge turntable in SCARLETT
was handsome, and in one way surprising to Japanese theatre-
goers. Japanese theatre has been using turntables for centuries,
but they usually present one setting, then lower the curtain
while they turn the full 180 degrees to present another. At curtain-up, the
new set is revealed. During the scenes, you hear hammering, unapologeti-
cally undiminished, as the next set is put in place. We had no hammering
in SCARLETT. We made the turning a feature, and the rise in sight of the
boat in mist and the sense of downriver motion worked — and this was
novel for the audience.

I love Kabuki and Bunraku. I rarely enjoy theatre now. I spent too much
time in dark auditoriums adjusting lights, and I'm too uncomfortable if
anything goes poorly. Recently I went to a benefit that featured a short
presentation. Going early into the auditorium, I became panicked. Would
it fill? I saw a lighting unit obviously out of focus, and I started to sweat.
But in the grand ritual of Kabuki, I do not know enough to perceive errors,
if there are any. I am a fresh audience, no longer an old warhorse. I like
the slow inevitability of the pace and the ferocity of the acting: everyone
stands at immediate risk of being beheaded. The music and narration are
grand and relentless. The costumes are gorgeous and the sets bright and
handsome, usually cartoonlike and eagerly sincere. I enjoy seeing prop men
in black walk onstage and hand someone a sword or teacup or maybe a
bloody hand or head. They are uncannily unseen if you're really into the
show — it's magic without sleight-of-hand.

In Bunraku, visible puppeteers tenderly guide their puppets toward glorious and often horrible fates. There is something so real, so dedicated, about a puppet: it has no other life, it does not take off its makeup and go home to a family in New Jersey. Its reality is absolute. Kabuki actors sometimes seem to me to be actors imitating puppets. One effective way to teach young actors is to hide their faces with masks. Thus hidden, they become free to lose their lives and become other lives — which is the idea of theatre, is it not?

WHAT I LEARNED

Theatre is so much: all the forms, all the insights, all the soaring emotions, sometimes the astonishment of pure beauty, sometimes pageantry — I'm embarrassed to try to describe all of it. I'm honored to have played a part in so many of these forms. Designers can wear these many hats. As I mentioned, it is now the fierce emotions revealed through ritual pageantry that have caught me, at this stage in my life.

I'm interested in teaching and training, and that's why this book is being written, so here is a story, funny and perhaps instructive, concerning ritual. Ten years after a small role in SCARLETT, Tetsuko Kuroyanagi had become one of Japan's great stars. She had a daily interview show. One evening, Leonora and I met her at her favorite sushi restaurant in Tokyo. We settled in, and after a few moments I asked Tetsuko if it was true that it takes eleven years to train a sushi chef. "That's what I've always heard," she said, "but let's ask the owner." He came over and sat with us. Tetsuko asked the question, and he answered "Yes, eleven years. See that boy," he said, pointing to an eight-year-old. "He learns to sweep the floor, two years. Then that boy" (who was ten or so) "clears the tables. Two years. That young man over there is learning to make salads. Two years. That young man comes down with us to the docks and learns how to pick the finest, the freshest fish. Two years. Then that young man, behind the counter, is learning to roll a good rice ball. One year. Finally, you see the last two years of training: the slicing, the combining everything. Eleven years."

"But," said Tetsuko, "what if there were some kind of strange national emergency and you had to train a chef quickly. Not a superior artist, but adequate. How long would that take?"

The owner thought for a long time. "Six weeks."

EXERCISE

Write down the outline of a book like this. Maybe you have not lived as long or had as good luck as I have. But instruct. Outline a chapter about your hopes in this profession. Do you aspire to be a designer, director, actor, critic, playwright? Why? Then name your heroes — who would you like to equal, even to meet and know? Why? What started you on this path? What luck or progress have you had so far? List encouragement and discouragement.

CHAPTER THIRTY-SEVEN

ℳr. ℬ.

THE YEAR I designed Todd Bolender and Frank Moncion's ballets was the year George Balanchine spent in Sweden because his wife, the fabled dancer Tanaquil Le Clercq, was disabled with polio. When he came back, Lincoln introduced us, and I designed his STARS AND STRIPES, danced to John Philip Sousa's music. "Elephant vomit," Mr. B. called it. But it's still in the repertoire more than sixty years later. I see it from time to time, but the original dancers, particularly Jacques d'Amboise and Melissa Hayden, are not there, and I have a perfectly ordinary and expected sense of loss, often called aging. I feel old also when I see A MIDSUMMER NIGHT'S DREAM and Eddie Villella is not soaring above the stage. When STARS AND STRIPES opened, a great flag, or at least the white-and-red stripes of it, would rise slowly during the finale. Stripe by stripe, on and on. This silk flag was fifty feet high, and from its opening position, folded on the floor, it could rise for a long time. When the house curtain fell, it was swiftly lowered halfway, and when the curtain rose for the bows, it had started up again, so the movement was seemingly without pause. Once, when I visited, the huge flag did not rise during the bows. The new stage managers had not been told of our simple trick. The lesson: visit.

Balanchine had an extraordinary eye, and he quickly saw anything that affected the dance. His comments were made in useful terms. Mr. B. had his Russian accent, of course (and I suspected he wanted to keep it), but his knowledge of our language was deep. For example: "David, clean up, big costumes, looks like washing machine." Or, "David, I see only legs, legs, a forest of legs." In that case, the light from above was edging the legs on both sides, and easing up on that and bringing in more light from one side would create the edging from just one side. He was good! As for self-confidence, if he really liked a ballet he had made, and the critics did not, he said, "Never mind, I'll keep in repertoire and will become classic."

When the sets were onstage, he was of enormous help, but he was not always persuaded that scenery was necessary. He wanted to see his dancers, his patterns: that was scenery enough. A stage picture with added scenery that I believed was an asset might, after a season or two, not reappear. The set for MONUMENTUM PRO GESUALDO was one of my prides. For EPISODES, one of the sets had been a white enclosure: white walls with a tall decorative pole set close to each corner. The poles mimicked the shapes of old door keys. This dance, with Martha Graham and Paul Taylor as guests, was not to be repeated, so I used two of the poles in MONUMENTUM. Placed just right, with one pole flying out at one moment, and the other then glowing with tiny lights, punctuated the space well—but for one season only, alas.

I remember the lovely dancing of Diana Adams. I always came to the theatre when she was dancing in PRODIGAL SON and painted her into her costume after she put it on. She was the enchantress. The ballet played in front of a drop copying Rouault's *The Old King,* and I touched it up from time to time. Lincoln, incidentally, danced in that ballet, or at least he entered and stood there in costume as the father as the spent prodigal climbed into his arms.

I designed ELECTRONICS, one of the first musical dance pieces that was composed exclusively with electronic devices. Violette Verdy danced in it, and called it "electronic-ca-ca." She seemed to me the most musical of the superb NYCB dancers. She did not merely dance beautifully to music, but she made it seem to flow out of her. This set was made of clear plastic and looked like trees or elephant legs, and at the end they jerked about the stage. An interesting set, but unloved—for a ballet that was unloved. Some wit called the set "Betty Grable's handbag." Because there was no work for the painters, it was also unloved by our union's business agent, and he appeared at the scene shop, assembled the painters, who were busy on other things, and roared, "Big hero, Hays—big-shot hero."

I was not Balanchine's personal friend. I do not know who was, if anyone. When he died, articles appeared flattering their authors with close
friendships that I doubt truly existed. Lincoln did not claim closeness. Balanchine was a man in most things, not a god, and he did man-like things:
cutting off his finger in his lawn mower was the least of it. He managed
his marriages badly; he referred to his ex-wives as "my old bags"— but he
honored Tanaquil, and maintained that marriage for many years, despite
his swain-like devotion to other women. But — as Eddie Villella said simply, "We loved him."

Lincoln showed up at my house one evening with an LP record of Fauré
compositions. "Listen to *Shylock* and *Pelléas et Mélisande*," he said, and
I did. I phoned him and told him how thrilled I was. The next day Balanchine appeared. "I want bring over Margot Fonteyn," he said, "and I
want to do dance for her in upside-down room." Lincoln followed in an
hour, and we went by cab to the Metropolitan Museum and he showed me
a marble table from the Renaissance in Bologna, if I remember correctly.
Typically, he said, "That's your set."

I began work, using the colors and many of the ornate details of the
inlaid table. Mr. B. was not pleased with my first model. "No, you have all
these angles; you try to give false energy — it's all Russian nineteen-thirties
'futurism.'" The surprise, he said, is that it's upside-down. The more the
room is exactly real and realistic, the more fantastic that it is upside-down.
On I worked, but we had much else to do. And there was no hurry. In a
month, I had another model. The marble table was planted on the floor,
which was now the ceiling. A crystal chandelier sprang up from the stage
floor. The full-height Italian Renaissance windows started at the top, a few
upside-down poplars visible through them, some upside-down paintings
between them. Mr. B. said that it was exactly right. "Fan*tastic*," was his
highest praise. "But," he added, "I'm not so happy now with music. Maybe
we commission score. Maybe, maybe Ravel." There I committed a blunder,
but it probably didn't matter. I said, "But Mr. B., isn't he dead?" Pause.
Mr. B. sniffed. It was a slight noise, easy to imitate. Make a sour-lemon-
taste expression, and when your face is all scrunched up, lift your chin and
sniff, just slightly. Just the sound; Mr. B. did not need a lemon face to do it.

That sniff ended the project. Totally. Just that small sound. It was never mentioned again. With hindsight, I do not believe it was a good concept. It's upside down — so what? A year later, Mr. B. used the Fauré score in JEWELS.

There was another project that took a sharp turn when I showed Mr. B. a model. (I made models, not drawings, of these settings. Since models do not store well, I have few records.) It was for Mozart's Divertimento no. 15. He studied the model. "David! Beautiful setting! I could put dancers here, and over there beautiful entrance for a pas de deux; and for second part, we have wonderful stars in sky. Fan*tastic*!" Pause. He stood back and gazed at the model. "What is it for?"

WHAT I LEARNED

I learned that I was able, if rarely, to enter into Mr. B.'s head. A few years ago, I moored my boat for a week at the ancient city of Moret in France. (I sailed on French canals.) At night, I listened to a CD of Strauss's *Four Last Songs* in Jessye Norman's rich, warm voice. The third night, and the third time through the recording, in the third song, I began to see angels rising from the music. Not Botticelli's or Raphael's Annunciation-style angels, beautifully feathered, but earth-colored angels rising from flowered ground. They were not full-bodied, but somewhat spread in space — that is, there were spaces between body parts, and the wing feathers floated, not always rooted. Almost transparent, these angels were clearly visible to me, and they were clearly in and from and rising out of and being born from the music. I had not gone crazy, nor was I dreaming or fantasizing. These were real images, forms coming from music — this is what I had been trained to do, what Balanchine had taught me to do. He made flesh from music, and here, at that moment, I saw it happening.

A few days later, I stumbled into an exhibition in a twelfth-century refectory that had been converted into an art gallery. On high pedestals, Bulgarian students had placed angels that were *exactly* like those in my head. Exactly. Frightening.

EXERCISE

Think about this: Does your respect for another person diminish because he or she speaks your native language with an accent? To you, is that person's thought process flawed? Beware. José Quintero and George Balanchine were not merely brilliant thinkers, but they also had huge vocabularies in English, their second language. Think of Joseph Conrad, who was enticed away from his native Polish because of his love of English. In his vast and deliberate exploration of the language, more extensive than native speakers, who often take it for granted, he became one of our finest voices.

CHAPTER THIRTY-EIGHT

Finale

THE SINGLE FINEST WORK I did for Mr. B. was the ballet BUGAKU, not to be confused with the Japanese dance gagaku of some years earlier. The design grew out of that heavy old platform, but it is airy and rising. The ballet is a fantasy of a Japanese wedding ceremony, with stately entrances and exits of attendants, and then the wedding couple is left alone for graceful coupling. It is erotic, but not to the point where my mother would have said, "That is *un*necessary." The idea of a bright platform with railings and a sense of suspension came easily. I used white ropes that seemed to suspend the railing. Again, for a brief moment I felt as if I had been lifted to the realm of creation where Balanchine lived. (Don't take that seriously.) The fascinating music was composed by Toshiro Mayuzumi, whom Lincoln had met in Japan. One woman asked Ron Bates how the musicians did it. "Well ma'am, they just rub balloons up and down their legs."

I'd like to retell a Balanchine story I relayed in a book about stage lighting, published many years ago. On nights when a new ballet was opening, Ronnie Bates, Mr. B., and I would stand at stage center, nervous. Yes, Mr. B. was nervous at these times. For himself? For his dancers? He would tell off-color jokes. The jokes were not that dirty — and not that good. This night was the opening of A MIDSUMMER NIGHT'S DREAM. My daughter, Julia, was too young to dance as a firefly with the older children — that would wait until the grand opening of the new stage at Lincoln Center. Involving children naturally involved their mothers, and once Mr. B. said, "Ce n'est pas la merde, ce sont les mères."

That night we all had our reasons to be nervous. Suddenly, mid-joke, Mr. B. straightened up. "I have idea. I know how to end ballet." We had a half-hour, but the curtain could wait five more minutes if necessary. Mr. B. explained his idea. Ronnie ran to get some thin, strong airplane cable; the flyman brought in a pipe; props brought some lampblack; the spotlight operator was called onstage; and I ran across the street to the diner to get some vinegar to clean the oily wire, which helps the lampblack to stick. We hung a loop of the wire from the pipe. In a few minutes our Puck was brought up from the dressing room. Mr. B. showed him how to step onto the loop of wire with a flourish that wrapped it securely around his arms. We rehearsed once; the dancers who would surround Puck gathered and watched; and that very evening, Puck sailed up into the sky as the curtain fell. No one said, "Gee, *now* he's got the idea? Where's he been?," and so forth. No, it was our Mr. B., and we were all with him — prop man, flyman, spotlight operator, Ronnie, me, and of course Puck. That's the way it was. If only it had lasted forever.

I said above earlier that parting with José was a moment of sadness that I cannot forget. So many of us have wandered sadly and uneasily since George died.

Now I plant roses. Anywhere I can find a sunny patch of soil, sandy perhaps, and if I'm going to hang around for a while, I plant roses. Mr. B. loved them. I still hear him saying, "David, speak more gently to your plants. Do not threaten them if they do not grow fast enough. Anyway, they only understand Russian."

EXERCISE

In the next chapter there is a thought about love. Read Carson McCuller's *The Ballad of the Sad Café.*

CHAPTER THIRTY-NINE

Encore

I ENJOYED TEACHING. Even though I've never been a communist or "fellow traveler," I and many others objected to signing a formal statement to that effect, so teaching for many of us ended at NYU. Then I taught graduate students at Columbia. One day I gave a test. Of the twelve students — graduate students, mind you — all recognized Michelangelo's *David*, but none recognized Goya's *Maya*, clothed or unclothed, or Canaletto or Guardi, two sources for a variety of plays. Only one recognized Vermeer. None had even heard of Hogarth. So much for the Restoration. This was the time of Peter Max and the feeling by some that history stifled the imagination.

The design profession can be rewarding, but to get work and get started often depends, like acting, on luck. As a teacher, I was uneasy leading these lambs to the slaughter — although those students I've encountered years later who adapted to other professions did not regret their years as waiters. I also taught classes of actors and directors with only a few designers mixed in, and enjoyed telling them what designers did and how to work with them — or at least understand them. I taught them to think carefully about settings, and to approach a play with careful regard for its surround. A simple example: Sartre's short play NO EXIT takes place in a room in hell. Fire and brimstone? No. Think again. Maybe wallpaper. I also taught seeing — looking sharply — because, again, the directors and producers and choreographers I enjoyed had one skill in common: marvelously keen eyes.

"How do you get ahead in this uncertain profession?" my students asked. I said the usual: Do dirty jobs eagerly; give an enema to a goat. Take all jobs as your start; you never know where they'll lead. But I added, to their surprise (I know I'm repeating this), "Learn to speak well. Form sentences not starting with 'well,' like television news people; use fewer 'ums;' and never use diluting drivel like 'like.'"

Will this profession continue in the face of the new devices, this upheaval when media companies are in turmoil, when publishers and bookstores are bowing to non-paper books? Yes it will. "The fabulous invalid," one nickname for live theatre, will gasp on. The difference between us and film is *time*. Peter Brook explains this in the best of all theatre books, his *The Empty Space*. You might think that live theatre is different because we stand alive in front of you, while the other media are on screens. True — but the real difference is *time*. What we do is happening *now*, in front of you, and the words coming from an actor's mouth (or hands, pardon me) are coming out for essentially the first time, or at least *now*. What is happening on film has already happened; it is in the past. It's as simple as that. We are rivaled by "live" TV and the Web, but they are still stuck on that screen. Time applies there as well. If I tune in to the box and miss the space shuttle landing, but immediately see a rerun of the event, I am not seeing the event but a canned rerun, and I'm disappointed. The held breath is gone; the 3–2 pitch has happened; the risk has passed. I'm watching a recording, an echo — not the event.

I want the actor to say his speeches face-to-face with me, in the same room or space. I am drawn to the campfire storytelling that has thrilled our species since fires were first lit. Seeing and hearing an actor's screen image repeat these same lines or stories is good, but it happened in the past. That excellent exploding chicken fooled no one, but it was in front of us *now*. Think how ordinary, how dull it would be, if we watched the balloon burst on the screen.

What's the future of scenery in all of this? Holograms? More spectacular film projections used as backgrounds? Will we wear special eyepieces to supply backgrounds? Perhaps we must do things that relate to film's sensational explosions or flights or underwater feats, because film expertise has bullied us into imitation? No — cheer up! Our accomplishments should be *better* than film's, because they should be imaginative transformations — and because they are *now*.

We can tell stories. We sent men to the moon; we have opposable thumbs. But is that why we are here? What distinguishes our species is our language and images that can preserve our events, real or imagined. Who is more real and more instructive to us: Richard Nixon, who lived a fascinating life in flesh, but is barely known by youngsters, or Hamlet, invented on paper, but always to be with us? We are storytellers. That is why we are here.

Live audiences participate. Film spectaculars are produced by myriad devices of animation and studio techniques, and hiding that magic, now taken for granted, is often the very point. But I enjoy the big dragon "live onstage" in front of me, because I see the feet of actors protruding from its four huge legs, and I delight in this kind of skill, even when it is simple. Actors have carefully rehearsed the dragon's walk. The dragon — the actual physical dragon — is carefully constructed; it is in the room with me. But there is also risk, and part of me is alert, because the dragon may fail. Perhaps I'm sitting on the edge of my seat with that concern. Isn't that the way I should be sitting? I enjoy the present dragon, and I am committed to it more than to the magnificent animal that film brilliance made in the past, with the many "takes" until it was perfected, with failures cut from the record, all altered digitally, then polished and frozen.

WHAT I LEARNED

What have I learned in all these years? I learned about love — the tortured love of the O'Neills; the innocent love of Butterfly; how Mimi, in her first aria, opens our hearts. (Our hearts are broken at the end of the opera, but first we must open them.) I was lucky; love is a glorious study. Pursued professionally, the course is for credit. My personal story, typically, has its ups and downs. A second marriage, after Leonora died, had love but failed: I believed love alone could accomplish too much.

I learned about loss, and was surprised and distressed that the death of a beloved cat caused as much pain as the death of human comrades. But, says my beautiful wife, Nancy Varga, who has worked as a grief counselor, "The death of a beloved animal opens the door to all grief." Perhaps we are duffel bags filling with grief, grief fed by growing sadness at our own approaching deaths. Is the pressure in this bag relieved from time to time by the death of an animal companion, a loss directly felt, without society's rituals and restraints? Do we also invent and tell the great stories to give us this relief? As I said before, we humans are storytellers. Yes, we walked on the moon; yes, Ben Edwards designed magnificent wallpaper. But that's what we do, not who we are.

Joseph Conrad talks of love and work and who we are in *The Mirror of the Sea*. He is speaking of the perfection of great southern-going ships, of "the love of perfected skill. For love is the enemy of haste; it takes count of passing days, of men who pass away, of a fine art matured slowly in the course of years. . . . Love and regret go hand in hand in a world of changes swifter than the shifting of the clouds reflected in the mirror of the sea."

That's what I learned, the space I inhabit, what I tried to do well. I sometimes did well and I sometimes failed, but I was a storyteller — a visual storyteller perhaps, a journeyman in our noble craft of telling the stories.

What is our greatest theme, our greatest story? Growing old and lost love. (That's another book.)

It's all about the actors who realistically portray imaginary lives. It's the girl Gelsomina in *La Strada*, or Violetta, or Laura in THE GLASS ME-NAGERIE, who all touch us deeply, who change us. Whether for film or television or stage, let's hope for perceptive directors who can wisely advise fine performers and then get the best light and angles on them, who will work with us, the designers, to give them the perfect place to be. What is the perfect place? For me, that will always be in the same room with us, at the same time.

And so, finally, finally:

When I took my little girl to the circus, I said at one moment, "Look, Julie, do you see that clown?"

"Yes, Daddy — but can he see me?"

Yes, my dear. He can.

INDEX

Note: Page numbers in *italics* indicate illustrations. Names of plays are in SMALL CAPITAL LETTERS; names of films and books are in *italics*.

DAVID HAYS, elected to the Theater Hall of Fame, has been designing sets for theatre productions ever since high school. While at Harvard University as an undergraduate, Hays became involved with the Brattle Theatre in Cambridge. After college, he received a Fulbright scholarship and apprenticed at the Old Vic theater in London. After returning to the States, Hays continued his education at the Yale School of Drama, and received a master's degree from Boston University. In New York, Hays worked as a highly respected set and lighting designer for more than fifteen years. He designed over fifty Broadway shows, as well as thirty ballets for George Balanchine. In 1967, Hays founded the National Theatre of the Deaf, and directed it for thirty years. He is an avid sailor, and he and his son, Daniel, became the first Americans to sail around Cape Horn in a vessel only twenty-five feet long. Together they coauthored the *New York Times* best-seller *My Old Man and the Sea* (1996). Hays lives with his wife Nancy in Chester, Connecticut.

ABOUT THE DRIFTLESS CONNECTICUT SERIES

The Driftless Connecticut Series is a publication award program established in 2010 to recognize excellent books with a Connecticut focus or written by a Connecticut author. To be eligible, the book must have a Connecticut topic or setting or an author must have been born in Connecticut or have been a legal resident of Connecticut for at least three years.

The Driftless Connecticut Series is funded by the
Beatrice Fox Auerbach Foundation Fund
at the Hartford Foundation for Public Giving.

For more information and a complete list
of books in the Driftless Connecticut Series,
please visit us online at
http://www.wesleyan.edu/wespress/driftless.